THE
BUSINESS
ALCHEMIST

THE

BUSINESS
ALCHEMIST

A ROAD MAP TO AUTHENTIC AND
INSPIRATIONAL LEADERSHIP

PILAR GODINO

HAY HOUSE

Carlsbad, California • New York City • London • Sydney
Johannesburg • Vancouver • Hong Kong • New Delhi

First published and distributed in the United Kingdom by:
Hay House UK Ltd, Astley House, 33 Notting Hill Gate, London W11 3JQ
Tel: +44 (0)20 3675 2450; Fax: +44 (0)20 3675 2451
www.hayhouse.co.uk

Published and distributed in the United States of America by:
Hay House, Inc., PO Box 5100, Carlsbad, CA 92018-5100.
Tel.: (1) 760 431 7695 or (800) 654 5126;
Fax: (1) 760 431 6948 or (800) 650 5115.
www.hayhouse.com

Published and distributed in Australia by:
Hay House Australia Ltd, 18/36 Ralph St, Alexandria NSW 2015.
Tel.: (61) 2 9669 4299; Fax: (61) 2 9669 4144.
www.hayhouse.com.au

Published and distributed in the Republic of South Africa by:
Hay House SA (Pty), Ltd, PO Box 990, Witkoppen 2068.
Tel./Fax: (27) 11 467 8904. www.hayhouse.co.za

Published and distributed in India by:
Hay House Publishers India, Muskaan Complex, Plot No.3, B-2,
Vasant Kunj, New Delhi – 110 070. Tel.: (91) 11 4176 1620;
Fax: (91) 11 4176 1630.
www.hayhouse.co.in

Distributed in Canada by:
Raincoast, 9050 Shaughnessy St, Vancouver, BC V6P 6E5.
Tel.: (1) 604 323 7100; Fax: (1) 604 323 2600

Text © Pilar Godino, 2013

The moral rights of the author have been asserted.

A catalogue record for this book is available from the British Library.

ISBN: 978-1-78180-101-7

With all of my love.

To Isabel Roldán – an example of strength and the embodiment of resilience, from whom I learned that no matter what setbacks and challenges I'm presented with, I need to get on with it since I'm ultimately the one in charge of the outcome.

To Carlos Godino – a generous and unconventional man and a free spirit from whom I learned thirst for knowledge and great curiosity for life.

Thank you both for your part in my life. I am blessed and privileged to have been born into such a family.

In loving memory of Sue Blake, who encouraged me to write, and supported me until the very end.

⤳ CONTENTS ⤳

~ FOREWORD ~

Leadership has been a passion of mine for many years. I first began intensively studying the skills of leadership more than 25 years ago when I spearheaded a major initiative on leadership development at the Italian car company Fiat in the late 1980s. I have written about the subject in numerous books and articles, and have taught hundreds of seminars throughout the world on various aspects of leadership.

Leadership is especially important in times of crisis, and it's probably one of the most important skill sets necessary for our businesses and our world today.

In *The Business Alchemist: A Road Map to Authentic and Inspirational Leadership*, Pilar Godino takes the critical subject of leadership, and how to develop it, a further step into new and important territory. Leaders of high-performance teams and world-class organizations are not 'bosses' or 'commanders', rather they are 'Alchemists', as Pilar points out.

This requires a special set of skills and abilities for recognizing and living your own excellence, managing relationships with elegance and compassion, and interacting effectively with others to move towards a vision of a rewarding future. As Pilar illustrates through practical exercises and case studies, these are skills that anyone can learn and which can make a powerful and positive impact on your business and on your life.

Alchemy was the medieval forerunner of chemistry, based on the transformation of matter and the attempt to convert base metals into gold. This is a powerful metaphor for the type of 'magic' that can happen at times in teams and organizations, and in our own lives. Under the proper conditions, ordinary circumstances and regular individuals are transformed into something in which the whole is truly greater than the sum of its parts.

Key to this type of Alchemy is a deeper connection to our own excellence. The 'soul' is a term used to refer to the deepest part of a person's nature, and is expressed as a special quality of 'emotional or intellectual energy or intensity'. Pilar provides road maps and methods by which you can connect more profoundly to your own excellence and express it more fully, taking you on a journey leading to greater self-expansion and freedom.

She provides simple, practical and powerful models, principles and steps for how to do it and become a more authentic and inspirational leader.

On a personal level, I initially met Pilar many years ago as a participant on a year-long course I was giving with my brother

John on Success Factor Modelling. The purpose of this course was to learn how to identify the 'differences that made a difference' between effective and average or poor performance. Pilar was an active and skilful participant, contributing greatly to the quality of the programme. This work on Business Alchemy and the Soul of Leadership is a clear demonstration that she has fully internalized the capacity for identifying and sharing those differences that make a difference in leadership.

Since that first connection, I have come to know Pilar as a friend and colleague, as well as a fellow trainer and coach. It is a pleasure to now welcome her as a fellow author. As you will discover for yourself, Pilar is a unique and extraordinary individual. She is a talented observer, an outstanding coach and a clear writer. As a person, she is energetic, proactive and intelligent, and brings a wonderful blend of clarity, compassion and humour to her work. All of these qualities shine through in this book.

I remember a meeting with Pilar some years ago and discussing strategies and offering tips about the process of writing a book based on her coaching and leadership work. I am very happy and grateful that this book is now here.

Robert Dilts
Founder, Dilts Strategy Group
Co-founder, NLP University

⤳ PREFACE ⤳

I've been giving leadership development seminars for many years and during the course of them I'm usually asked whether I can recommend a book that supports their content. My answer has always been: 'I can recommend good leadership books, but the material I've just shared with you has not yet been written in a book.'

The Business Alchemist is my response to this need. Through its pages I share with you what I've learned about people, how to build strong and long-lasting strategic relationships, and how to address, in the most efficient way possible, each person you want to influence – whether they are a member of your team, a peer, your boss or a friend.

Drawing on what I've witnessed during more than 7,000 hours of one-to-one coaching conversations, I write about business leaders and their different attitudes and styles, and offer some amazing new perspectives on the implementation of vision and strategy.

Through working with people who've embraced and put into practice the concepts explained in the following pages, I've watched ordinary managers become excellent leaders, and I've seen excellent leaders become extraordinary ones – become Business Alchemists.

This book aims to do the following things:

- Challenge some of your assumptions and leadership habits.

- Invite you to discover something about yourself that you didn't know before.

- Serve you with a fresh, clever, and solid standpoint from which to motivate and appreciate your team.

- Increase your confidence in 'managing up'.

- Add a new dimension to your leadership.

- Encourage you to explore a leadership style that improves results and relationships through quick and effective conversations.

- Awaken your awareness of using leadership as a source of generous, powerful, and transformative wealth.

- Generate Business Alchemy.

- Enable you to accomplish all the above with joy – while having fun!

This book is about building *character*. It's about developing the generosity of spirit necessary to grow – not only within yourself, but in helping others develop too. It's about creating a safe environment, or ambience, where you can develop your immediate reports so that they, in turn, can aid and develop each individual in the team.

It's about building and maintaining strong relationships, and creating a culture to which people want to belong: a culture where we are all midwives of growth.

This book is about Business Alchemy – where the leader, as the Alchemist, brings out the gold in his or her people, while being personally transformed in the process.

∼ INTRODUCTION ∼

Can you remember being amazed by the sight of a rainbow? I can – and I was truly surprised by what I saw. I was in an aeroplane, looking out of the window and daydreaming, when there it was: a perfectly formed rainbow, strongly defined by the sharp contrast of its bright colours against the soft white background of the clouds.

But this rainbow was different from any I'd seen before – not only in the strength of its colours, and in the long duration of the experience, but also in its *shape*, because, seen from high up in the air, a rainbow is not the familiar arch but a perfectly formed circle. On Earth, the angle at which we view a rainbow allows us to see only half of it.

In much the same way, when we're involved in the everyday running of a business, our standpoint may result in us seeing only a *partial* view of it. *The Business Alchemist* offers you the opportunity to take a sky-high look at the full circle of leadership, so when you're grounded in day-to-day business matters, you'll also keep a broad perspective and expand the spectrum of your leadership.

THE CHANGING FACE OF LEADERSHIP

In the last few decades there have been dramatic changes in our daily lives. Advances in digital technology have enabled us to 'go global'; we have an urge to communicate, and many new things are suddenly within our reach. In business, organizations are now facing different kinds of challenges, and, as the workplace has become more demanding, leadership has had to evolve rapidly.

In today's high-powered corporate world leaders are developing their people not only practically, but also *emotionally*. By enhancing the self-esteem of individual members of staff, and prizing values such as authenticity, trust, transparency, collaboration, and learning from each other's strengths, their teams are performing more strongly, faster and more efficiently, and delivering greater results.

Leaders now work under enormous pressure, and as a result it has become necessary for them to embrace a new philosophy. The old way of telling people what to do and how to do it is giving way to a more creative method of working: delegating with trust and helping staff to grow, both professionally and personally.

If leaders are to be successful in this philosophy, though, it's essential that they've reached a certain level of personal development themselves. In order to be happy and successful in developing staff, leaders need a generosity of spirit. In the same way that when we educate our children we encourage them to improve – in the hope that they'll become better than us over time – so too in leadership it's important to adopt this approach with staff, and to celebrate when that day arrives.

You may be interested in exploring leadership in a new and profound way – by examining different and interesting angles that resonate with you, and experiencing an alternative view. Or you may prefer to affirm what you're already doing well – validating all the things you know, and continuing to improve at your own pace while integrating a modern approach into your leadership and keeping a firm hold on things.

The complexity of matrix organizations puts their functional leaders in the delicate situation of having to influence people who don't report to them directly. If you want to influence not only your direct and/or functional reports but also your peers and your boss, the insights in this book will add depth and awareness, and increase the effectiveness of your leadership.

THE ROLE OF THE LEADER IS TO LEAD

'You can cut a tree twice as quickly if you invest some extra time in sharpening the axe.'

There is practical wisdom in this proverb, to which I add my own: 'You will be twice as effective and in control when you know where, how, and when to hit that tree.'

The more you throw yourself into the insights and processes contained in this book, the more you'll get out of it, and the more you'll take charge of your leadership style – leaving behind any struggle to understand people, and any difficulty in delegating, and allowing you to open up to other choices.

I've coached more than 700 people, including senior leaders in corporate and public organizations, entrepreneurs, sports competitors and those in the arts. I've coached coaches, successful musicians and performing magicians; I've coached teachers, house husbands, housewives and students. They were all very different people, with contrasting views, yet it's what I found they had in common that propelled me to write this book.

In coaching leaders I've learned about many things: the frustrations caused by demotivated employees, the heavy weight of lack of commitment in some of the workforce, the near exhaustion resulting from extended periods of working long hours, the constant struggle with peers, and the difficulty of managing upwards.

And from the workforce I've learned about the frustrations of working for a boss who has no vision and no manners, and who treats others 'as if they were stupid'; about the eternal dissatisfaction of 'not being allowed to do as much as I could', and the perception that 'you have to be a bastard to get a promotion'.

No matter how much we attempt to leave our emotions out of the workplace, in times like the one we're living in – in which pressure is high, deadlines are plenty, and the hours seem to fly by – it's inevitable that we'll bring an emotional charge to our work. Whether you're a leader who is exasperated by people who aren't giving their best, or a worker who has given up trying, fed up with a boss who doesn't extract even a pinch of what you could offer, you are just as frustrated as each other.

But it's the responsibility of the *leader* to break the status quo.

My View of Leadership

My view of leadership is broad and analytical. It comes from observing diverse perspectives, with a special focus on the experiences of all the amazing leaders I've coached. From my seat I've seen, heard, felt and known their passion for self-improvement, and their courageous mind-opening processes. I've had the great privilege to witness their commitment to self-awareness and team development; their loyalty, care and love for the job, the organization and the people; and how far it's possible to go in leadership.

The role of the leader is to lead his or her people to accomplish the various stages towards the final vision of the organization. In doing this, they use motivation as one of the means to:

- Lead the organization using vision – communicating the vision and strategic planning, and creating and distributing the structure.

- Lead the people by engaging and motivating the team, creating the desired atmosphere, and achieving the chain of targets to arrive at the vision.

Until recently, leadership was solely about directing and achieving, and the style of leadership was competitive and solitary ('Me for me, on my own against the world'); in some types of organization, this is still the case. Increasingly, though, there's the beginning of a recognition that leadership is not only about skills, but about *character*.

Cooperative or collaborative leadership is regenerative and takes things further. In order to be the new kind of leader – to lead with authority in a cooperative and generative fashion – it's necessary to combine great character with generosity of spirit.

The Business Alchemist will help you not only to retain talent and minimize staff turnover, but also – if developed to the full – encourage and distribute talent to the appropriate level across your organization, therefore realizing individual and team potential and raising the levels of job satisfaction exponentially.

In addition, the book talks about motivation – not as the purpose, but as the consequence of transformation. When your presence makes people want to be better, when your influence makes people feel important, you become their role model. Subsequently, they want what you want, and they want to follow you. In essence, they will want to *be* like you.

Pilar Godino
December 2012

PART 1

ARE YOU AN INSPIRING LEADER?

Inspiration means to inhale, to breathe in. When we're inspired by someone we breathe in the subject matter of inspiration — we make it ours. This is why we often want to be like the person who inspires us, or want to become them.

~ INTRODUCTION ~

Can you think of a person you knew early on in your life –
when you were a child or an adolescent – who inspired you?
Someone with whom you felt special, important, unique, or
extraordinary? Someone who, when you were in their company,
made you feel good about yourself, and therefore made you
want to attempt things you'd never tried before? Perhaps it was
a relative, a teacher or a friend's relative? Maybe as I tell you
about one of those special people in my life, you can think
about who yours might be.

I come from an extremely large family, so I had plenty of
relatives around me as I was growing up. My uncle, Jose Maria,
and his wife Tere have always been very welcoming people.
They are highly academic and dynamic, yet warm and loving.
My uncle had an amazing gift: each of his 67 nephews and
nieces believed they were his favourite. A highway, harbour
and bridge architect, he was also a university professor who
made each of his pupils feel they were the best. He was a

man of great intelligence and accomplishments, yet he always showed great humility.

I had the privilege of spending long spells of time with my uncle's family, because his daughters are the same age as me. During mealtimes, he would ask questions so we could show how much we knew. Afterwards he'd come to me, and as he gently poked my nose with his index finger, he'd look into my eyes and say with a smile: 'That was brilliant, show me more tomorrow.' Obviously I was very motivated to learn more so I could continue to share what I'd learned, and to this day, learning and sharing are my highest motivators.

As you think now about the person who inspired you when you were younger, what was it about him or her that made it so?

- Were you listened to?

- Did they show an interest in *you*?

- Was this person setting all their wisdom aside and making space for you to shine?

- Did you want to offer this person the best you had?

- Were you motivated to do what was required to shine again?

Now think about someone who inspired you *later* in your life; what was it about them that made it so?

- Did they display qualities that you possess? Or qualities you would *want* to have?

⚲ Did you have the desire to become like them? To develop their qualities?

⚲ If so, did they encourage you, or did you encourage yourself?

In fact, people who inspire us don't *give* us anything of theirs – they are naturally triggering our self-value mechanism and pushing our self-worth buttons. Whether they do this by encouraging us to show what we already have, or simply by displaying some qualities we want to develop, they are catalysts for growth. They bring the spark to ignite something we already have, however dormant. Most of the time, they're unaware of the wonderful impact they have on our lives. This is true Alchemy at work.

~ 1 ~

AN INSPIRING
LEADERSHIP STYLE

Inspiring leaders hold the key to unlocking dormant talent – enabling others to find their own approach.

Being aware of the impact we have on other people gives us a stronger basis for choosing our behaviour. For example, when we know that certain things we do have a positive effect on others, we can choose to repeat them purposefully, and as often as required.

One key way to spark people into feeling good about themselves is *to listen with interest*. When we show that we care on a daily basis, we inspire self-confidence in others. If, as a leader, you show interest in your people, they'll want to show *you* the best they can offer. And they'll naturally want to carry on being important to you, even if their ideas are not implemented straight away.

Here, one of my clients, a marketing director, talks about how we can inspire each other in the workplace:

⟶ BUSINESS ALCHEMY IN ACTION ⟵

In the past, I'd never comment on peers' shortcomings because I feared being perceived as intrusive, interfering, or critical of their work. I tried to mind my own business.

During my experience of becoming a Business Alchemist I was surprised to realize that, in trying to avoid conflict, I was actually *bringing* greater conflict into my business. With this realization – and after going deeper into knowing myself and my needs – I decided immediately to become more candid in conversations when necessary, and to adopt a policy of strict transparency.

There were three outcomes following the above revelation. The first was to recognize the bigger picture – that my peers' business is *my* business, and we're all in pursuit of the same goal. The second was to learn that my peers respect and welcome my input into the business, and find my feedback helpful. The third was that my peers embraced this approach, which resulted in many inspiring exchanges between us.

As soon as I started to act on these changes, my leadership grew to a higher level. As a consequence I now have a greater influence on the business and increased recognition from the organization.

When we believe in people, they give of their best. This understanding is one of the basic principles of coaching, which makes it an essential component in any inspiring leadership style and in Business Alchemy itself.

INTRODUCING BUSINESS ALCHEMY

Business Alchemy is a concept of leadership that recognizes the importance of finding a balance between *directing*, *mentoring* and *coaching*. It encompasses all three of these leadership styles and, since it's the most complete, it's therefore the most effective at developing people. Business Alchemy is based on knowledge, experience and wisdom.

Directing, mentoring and coaching provoke different reactions in the individuals you lead:

- ▰ **Directing** is about *telling* others what to do and how to do it – based on your idea of how a task could or should be done.

- ▰ **Mentoring** is about *showing* people how to do what needs to be done – based on your own experience of the role and what works and what doesn't.

- ▰ **Coaching** is about *asking* questions to bring awareness, to boost confidence and to encourage people to find their own approach.

Or, to put it another way:

Directing *tells*

Mentoring *shows*

Coaching *asks*

Business Alchemy *develops*

There's currently a trend that favours 'coaching' leadership over 'directive' leadership. However, there's an advantage in being proficient in both styles, since it enables us to adapt our approach to the individual and the circumstances.

The use of coaching as a key component of Business Alchemy means giving up the traditional way of telling people what to do and how to do it, and giving way to a more creative method of working: delegating with trust and helping staff to grow, both professionally and personally. In the latter scenario, a leader doesn't automatically present his or her solution to a problem (whether the solution is known or not), but acts more as a sounding board for other people's ideas; as a supporter or reviewer of those ideas – sometimes monitoring plans before they are formally implemented – or as a source of insights derived from a broader experience.

Ultimately, it's advantageous for an organization to create an atmosphere in which ideas sparkle and are listened to. This stimulates other possible ways of working while giving people permission to be creative – whether or not their suggestions are followed through. It also brings out the courage in individuals to be themselves and reveal their best, thus generating new ideas, adding a richer perspective, and offering a diverse range of solutions.

THE RIPPLE EFFECT OF BUSINESS ALCHEMY

The most successful organizations are educating their leaders and managers to establish coaching-style conversations with their direct and functional reports. This starts with leaders at the top and is followed by the next level of seniority and so on – therefore rippling down through the organization. This is especially important in the case of functional leadership, where the power of influence, rather than power for its own sake, is the key to motivating others to succeed.

For this ripple effect to take place, it's vitally important to monitor each person's progress and provide them with regular feedback – positive or otherwise. This ensures that everyone maximizes his or her contribution to the desired result. How regularly feedback is provided will depend on the level of development already attained by each person, and can be agreed *a priori*. Feedback provides the critical link between day-to-day activity and the achievement of the development goal. In Chapter 12, we look in more detail at how to provide the most effective feedback in a given situation.

THE BENEFITS OF BUSINESS ALCHEMY

The fact that in these financially challenging times organizations are investing in creating a less directive culture suggests there must be benefits to it. Successful leaders in pioneering organizations such as RBS, Merck & Co, Diageo, KPMG, Danone, Aviva and Vodafone, to name just a few, are committed to helping direct reports achieve performance goals through personal development. They are managing performance by listening, asking, guiding, integrating, and providing support.

Business Alchemy is rapidly becoming a key component in the achievement of objectives. It is being used as an ongoing process of communication, feedback and support, and as an effective way of assisting individuals to achieve their goals.

Below are some of the benefits of Business Alchemy, for both leaders and staff:

The Benefits for Leaders

- It shifts responsibility from manager to report.

- It enhances direct report learning, sense of responsibility and commitment.

- It clarifies performance expectations.

- It creates and maintains positive working relationships – and builds trust.

- It improves the performance of staff in their current role.

- It supports the efficient delegation of tasks.

The Benefits for Teams

- It motivates people to be themselves.

- It encourages independence, initiative and decision-making.

- It provides recognition for individual accomplishments and strengths.

- It helps staff to trust themselves to overcome obstacles, and increases their confidence.

- It addresses areas that need improvement by setting steps for continuous development.

~ 2 ~

USING YOUR
LEADERSHIP PLATFORM

'Leadership is ultimately about creating a way
for people to contribute to making something
extraordinary happen.'

Alan Keith, Lucas Digital

Business Alchemy is about leading with purpose, with
awareness, and with responsibility. It's about being a catalyst
for the growth of the people around you. It's about using
your *leadership platform* to create and maintain excellent
relationships. And it's about *self*-leadership, as well as leading
your people and the organization.

WHAT'S A LEADERSHIP PLATFORM?

When I first met Stuart Fletcher, then president of the
international division of Diageo, the world's leading premium
drinks business, I immediately witnessed his commitment to
his team, and what he said had a profound effect on me:

'When I first became president of Diageo International at the age of 47 I thought I'd made it. But almost immediately, I felt privileged in realizing that I wasn't at the top but rather at the base; I wasn't at the pinnacle, but I was the support. This position gave me the opportunity to use the leadership platform to serve my team, to develop people, to give more.'

I was impressed and deeply touched by the humility of Stuart's message, and by his warmth and approachability. It was the first time I'd heard of the concept of a 'leadership platform', and I interpreted it as the whole space, status, power and influence that surrounds a position such as that held by Stuart, as well as the privilege and duty it entails. Stuart had found that his responsibility was not only to develop the business, but also to turn his leadership into an opportunity to develop his people.

The Alchemical nature of Stuart's leadership is borne out by the experience of one of his directors, Ron Anderson, when he reported to him. Here's Ron's story:

⚜ BUSINESS ALCHEMY IN ACTION ⚜

I've spent most of my career working in a competitive and combative environment. My early professional reputation was based on high performance and tough leadership. I wanted to be seen as invincible – always in control, always up, never afraid, having all the answers (or so I thought), keeping my distance. I felt that I was fair, but some others would've said I was harsh.

As a child I'd convinced myself that showing any kind of weakness would lead to failure, so I spent my adult life presenting a false façade to the world. I never really thought about my personal style because I'd always been successful. What I didn't realize was that no one knew who I *really* am – and that this fact was getting in the way of my progress.

My wake-up call came when Stuart Fletcher, my boss at the time, set me on the journey of leadership development. I've had many good managers in my working life, but Stuart got to me in a way that would come to make a profound difference. He pushed me to work closely with a coach, who really understood what I was about.

During the coaching, I had a deep look at myself. I reflected on the impact of my behaviour, and on the brutality of my leadership style. I realized that I was tolerated because my performance was good, and I delivered great results, but unless people truly knew me, there would always be doubts about me. Yes, I produced lots of good people, but I also wore through them like there was no tomorrow.

I started to open my mind to the realization that I'd get better results by working with people rather than driving them. I knew I had a knack of understanding people and getting close to them, so I asked myself, *Why don't I do that all the time? What's stopping me?* I then experienced a major breakthrough. My professional ambition to join the executive board changed to wanting to be the best leader I could be, based on who I am, as opposed to who others think I am, or who I'd pretended to be in the past.

I had a bit of a watershed moment when I shared my personal breakthrough with the executive board and 90 other business leaders within the organization. I'd been asked to talk about my leadership journey, so I declared out loud that the *real* Ron was this guy – the one who cares about this and is sorry about that; the one who really loves working with his boss and appreciates all that he has received.

In sharing this insight with others on the leadership team, I felt a huge sense of relief. It gave me great freedom; it changed how the leadership group thought of me; and it gave me permission to be myself. Above all, it allowed me to be a better leader – more powerful within Diageo. It may have had some impact on getting me to executive level, but above all it changed my leadership style forever.

As I stopped pretending, I made huge strides in my relationships, and I was able to begin making changes in the business that I couldn't have achieved before – either because I'd had adversarial relationships with no respect, or because I'd not been prepared to risk failure. I've found huge value in not fearing failure – in allowing myself to be vulnerable and human.

I now feel able to help those who aren't performing to their full potential to perform better. I encourage them to 'be themselves'. My aspiration is to enable people to achieve things that they didn't think they could. That may sound rather trite, but it's something I get a real kick out of.

What I say now to other leaders is this: 'Take a risk, be yourself, and test out the leader you want to be.' The journey to leadership mastery is an ongoing process of learning that involves taking some level of personal risk.

Ron's personal transformation was the direct result of the Business Alchemy of his leader's approach. Embracing a culture of development and growth and then cascading it from the top down makes it as powerful for the organization as for each individual.

Although the ideal scenario would be for a corporation to endorse this leadership approach as a strategic initiative with support from the top, it's also possible for each leader to achieve amazing results by using their leadership platform consciously from whatever level they're at. Whether your leadership role is linear or functional, there's the opportunity to develop your team and build win-win relationships – with your peers, with your boss and with the stockholders – by understanding and using the Language of Influence. This is explored in depth in Chapters 6 and 7.

THE TRAITS OF ALCHEMIC LEADERSHIP

I'm going to assume that you've already attained the leadership and management skills necessary for your leadership position.

So we'll therefore explore the art of creating and maintaining win-win relationships, leading and influencing people, and self-leadership.

At the heart of Alchemic leadership lie *character, charisma* and *self-leadership.* Let's take a look at these in turn.

Character

This is shown through composure, strength, confidence, clarity, the ability to say 'no', and standing tall during times of difficulty.

Charisma

This is evident through charm, appeal, magnetism, allure, and presence.

It's possible for you to boost either of the elements above; you just need to choose, through self-leadership, which of them you want to develop and how far you want to go.

Self-leadership

This is the discipline of knowing and guiding yourself according to your own purpose and values. Knowing yourself is the foundation upon which to build character, and from where to display charisma. It's the foundation of Alchemic and purposeful leadership, and encompasses the ability to inspire and influence, to develop others, and to act as a catalyst for change. Self-leadership requires self-enquiry, listening to the answers, and becoming aware of your emotional state, your values and standards, and your impact on other people.

EXERCISE: INCREASE YOUR SELF-AWARENESS

~~~

Take a moment now to assess your self-leadership by noting your response to the questions below. Doing this mentally will increase your self-awareness, but making a physical note of your answers is important, too, because you'll be able to refer back to them as you read through the rest of the book.

➢ What makes me want to get up every morning?

➢ What's important for me at work?

➢ What are my strengths?

➢ What qualities do I bring to my position?

➢ How would I 'sell' myself?

➢ What qualities would I expect in someone holding a position like mine?

Now make a list of the strengths, qualities and characteristics of your *ideal* leader. (This could be someone known to you, or not – it could even be your ideal self.)

Once you've done this, note your response to the following questions:

➢ What do you think is important to your 'ideal leader'?

➢ What are their values?

➢ What do they stand for?

(If thinking of your ideal self, always consider and listen to your values and beliefs before drawing a picture of the person you aspire to be.)

~~~

Establishing Your Development Goal

Once you've completed the exercise, look at your responses and draw your conclusions:

- Where's your leadership now? *This is your starting point.*

- What's your leadership development goal? Where do you want your leadership to be? *This will be your finish line – your development goal.*

Once you've established your starting point and finish line, you're ready to build on your strengths and reduce any gaps you've found. There's no need to be strong in every area – no one is – but you may choose to improve on what's important for you. It's important you do this in accordance with your values and ethics, and in agreement with your very core.

Here, one of my clients now recalls his 'Aha' moment – when he realized the importance of showing his true Self to others:

⇀ BUSINESS ALCHEMY IN ACTION ⇀

It's ironic that I work in a sales environment and think constantly about product and organizational image, while underplaying my own brand – my persona. (In my country's culture it's common to think that, although we may be brilliant, it's up to other people to see it; if they fail to do so, it's their problem.) Now I understand that it doesn't really matter what you truly are, because unless you show it, other people won't see it.

A few days ago, a group of young colleagues from other departments were joking that all sales people are mavericks. A young woman from sales complained at this, saying, 'We're not really like that.' She was surprised when I replied, 'That might not be how we are, but if that's how we show ourselves to be, that's how they see us.'

First impressions count because we fix our beliefs about other people very quickly – the first few moments of any meeting are vital. This has been the biggest adjustment I've had to make: transforming my image from the ogre or the bully into the influential, smooth-spoken sales director I'm known as today, while realizing that I have to give people more than one chance before I form a definite impression of them.

LISTENING TO YOURSELF AND OTHERS

It's important to consider what has stopped you so far from being the leader you want to be. If it's simply been a lack of awareness, you can now start to steam ahead. But if it's something else, what is it?

By listening deeply to ourselves we get to know who we really are. We can identify our own values, beliefs and goals, and behave in accordance with them. This is the road to emotional maturity. And it's beneficial to keep up the self-enquiry as we continue to grow.

By listening deeply and purposefully to others, we get to know their values and goals, too. This enables us to find common ground and build productive win-win relationships. However long it takes to learn to listen with purpose – both to ourselves and to others – the reward is a whole new level of communication and problem-solving, because we acquire the ability to see a situation simultaneously from multiple points of view while knowing our own strengths.

> **If you want to get the best out of someone, you first need to believe that the best is inside them.**

BUILDING CHARACTER AND RADIATING CHARISMA

A leadership position brings power, and with that, responsibility. Embedded in the capacity to lead lies the ability to influence, which is deeply linked to character and charisma.

To display inner character automatically, and with composure, we need to know who we are. We need to be comfortable in our own skin, and to know our worth and the value we bring to the business and to the people around us. Then we can project our true Self, and give without fear. The word 'charisma' comes from the Greek meaning 'gift'. This is why we display charisma when we *give* of ourselves to others; when we are present. The opportunity to give stems from first knowing who we are and what we have to offer.

I invite you to contemplate self-leadership and giving a little further now by asking yourself the following questions:

- Am I using my leadership platform in the way I consider optimum?

- Could I do more?

- What motivates me?

- How is my relationship with my team members?

- Am I acting as a catalyst for others to develop?

- Have I created an environment of trust?

- Do I allow people to make mistakes?

- What is currently working well and what is not?

- Do I want to get different results?

- Do I want to do anything differently?

MASTERING SELF-LEADERSHIP

Business Alchemy starts from within, which is why it's so important to master self-leadership in order to become the Alchemist for others. When you are thinking about your leadership, consider the following points:

Your Leadership Style

Understand what represents you and what doesn't. You are unique, and what suits others does not need to suit you, too. If you understand yourself, and your values and goals, it's essential to honour that.

The Value of Authenticity

Building on the point above, the more we're true to ourselves, the more we bring to the people around us, and to the organization.

The Need for Trust

Creating an environment of trust, where people are allowed to make mistakes and be human, is part of the process of learning.

Using Your Leadership Platform to Develop Others

Consider the ways in which you can encourage others to be genuine and bring out the best in themselves.

The Importance of Motivation and Commitment

Commitment and motivation go hand in hand and they are vibrant and infectious. Getting any member of your team to commit will contribute to creating an energetic atmosphere that invites other team members to want to work.

THE OBSTACLES TO ALCHEMIC LEADERSHIP

As a leader you face both *internal* and *external* challenges. External challenges include a difficult financial climate; nervous stakeholders; a boss who looks over your shoulder all the time, who doesn't listen, or who depends too much on your opinion; peers who want to engage in a power struggle, or who envy you or want to compete all the time; and team members who are impossible to motivate or engage, are there for an easy ride, are headstrong and will not follow because they 'know better', or who get hurt easily and find you too pushy or offensive.

You may also face some internal challenges, such as time management, prioritization, stress, managing your emotions, saying 'no', having a life outside work, lack of motivation and self-belief, difficulty making some types of decisions, taking risks, and so on.

Whether the challenges you face are external or internal, the obstacles preventing you from excelling stem from *within*. They may be disguised in many shapes and forms, but they are still inside you. In essence, everything returns to the need for personal perspective: remembering that the rainbow of leadership is not the single arc that's visible on Earth, it's the whole radiant circle of potential that's visible from the air.

As a leader you have so much more to offer than what's visible on the surface. The three areas where this lack of perspective manifests most often are:

⌐ Recognition and Limited View of Ambition = Relationship with Ego

⌐ Appearing Human vs the Superhero Syndrome = Relationship with Vulnerability

⌐ Trusting Others = Relationship with Control

RECOGNITION AND LIMITED VIEW OF AMBITION

I've found many times in my career that people tend to minimize their impact by paying too much attention to their need for recognition. To a varying degree, this has been as true for me as it has for almost every person I've encountered.

Let me share a clear example of this in David's story:

~ BUSINESS ALCHEMY IN ACTION ~

David, a newly appointed senior leader and a talented speaker, was preparing for an important presentation to 400 people. In our session, I asked him what his intention was for the talk and he replied: 'I want them to know that this project is in the right hands.'

His response puzzled me because I was expecting to hear something more closely related to the project, the message of the presentation, or to the people he was presenting to. I was concerned that because David was setting the main focus on proving himself, his audience would switch off within seconds.

As our session progressed, David came to realize his true intention was to get the audience engaged in the project – for them to make it their own, and feel they were part of it. For that he needed to deliver the message with a different emphasis. This realization helped him change his focus from self-image and recognition to engaging others.

After he'd made the presentation, David sent me an SMS saying: 'I've just given the best presentation of my life.' He realized that being recognized as the best person to head the project was not his true goal, but rather the consequence of aiming further and beyond his ego. It was a turning point in his leadership perspective.

This scenario is not that different from the experience Ron shared with us at the beginning of the chapter. We all have within us the capacity to restrict the scope of our ambition when we confuse it with our need for recognition. Whatever level we're at, we need to justify our position or prove our worth, and this ambition is restrictive because it is ego based.

When we expand the circle of ambition to encompass a broader aim that involves the needs and fulfilment of others – when we reach beyond ourselves – we're more likely to succeed. This is the paradox.

I've come across this dilemma, in different manifestations, with at least 95 per cent of my clients. No matter how good they are at business strategy, and regardless of how high up in their organization's hierarchy they sit, at times they lose sight of the full circle of the rainbow.

During childhood, our ego is important for survival; in adolescence and early adulthood it's what drives us to succeed. Having an ego is part of the human condition. We all have one; even the most evolved person on the planet has an ego. The difference lies in the relationship we have with it – in recognizing it, knowing its habits and when it's likely to strike – and giving it the appropriate space.

So, are you in charge of your ego or is your ego in charge of you? All egos want to be in charge sometimes, and many times they succeed. If we recognize the ways of the ego, we have a bigger chance of making our decisions from a place of strength.

The main manifestations of ego are fear, self-pity, envy, the need for recognition, and power games. If we listen to our needs, and to our emotions, we can use our ego to show us when and where we need to grow above it. Our ego can be our greatest ally in helping us grow and develop.

APPEARING HUMAN VERSUS THE SUPERHERO SYNDROME

One of the most difficult things for leaders to achieve in any area of their lives is being at ease in asking for help. This uncomfortable action often leads to the Superhero Syndrome, where a leader ends up standing alone. I have seen this approach time and time again in leaders who believed that being in *total* control at all times, and having all the answers, was part of their job description. They never considered asking their boss for support for fear that he or she might think less of them as managers or leaders.

This attitude seems to stem from beliefs held about personal strength and duty, and the assumptions made about the consequences of showing vulnerability. In leaders, the consequences of the Superhero Syndrome are self-pressure and excessive stress – combined with a less-than-human image which, when encountered by reports, makes them appear unapproachable, thereby creating a vicious circle.

In the next chapter, we'll be looking at beliefs and their consequence in our lives and our leadership. In the meantime, take some time now to think about what strength means to you and make a note of your response. If you want to achieve more with this exercise, you can add dictionary descriptions of strength, leadership, duty, and vulnerability.

TRUSTING OTHERS

Many leaders and managers have difficulty with delegation – it's natural for them to want to be in control. Whether it's a matter of not trusting others enough, or a matter of habit, the effort required to overcome this tendency is one of the most rewarding, since prioritization and time management also improve as a consequence.

We create difficulties in this area as a result of our relationship with the ego, and/or the assumptions we've made in our lives. As long as we believe that 'if you want a job done well, you must do it yourself', and as long as we strive for perfection (whatever that means to us), we make delegation difficult. Some of the assumptions that are embedded in us come from our culture, and the pieces of 'old wisdom' that are passed down through the generations.

However, it's possible to rise above all this by bringing to your leadership your own wisdom; expanding your horizon to include others, and aiming wider and further than ever before. A Business Alchemist adds the power of influence through character and persuasion – via charisma, faith and passion – to the ability to direct and guide the self and others.

PART 2

SELF-LEADERSHIP

Excellent leadership starts with
knowing and leading oneself.

⤳ INTRODUCTION ⤳

As you know, an essential element of leadership is creating and handling challenges. I've found that the strongest challenge most leaders face is breaking through their own superficial surface to get to know the person hidden behind the familiar façade – the true 'I' – and then using this newfound knowledge to their advantage, development and growth. Overcoming this obstacle takes both their leadership and their lives to places they'd previously overlooked, considered out of reach, or did not even dream of.

This part of *The Business Alchemist* endeavours to clear away the cobwebs from areas of your leadership that get overlooked while your focus is solely on business and current targets. It will consciously reawaken your mind, and your inner resources, by challenging your mindset, your tendencies, your assumptions and your convictions. This will reposition you to choose what's most advantageous for your leadership, your life and your future.

In the next two chapters, I share with you an insight into how the mind works, how to look for the source of your inner obstacles, and how to turn whatever you find to your favour by mastering your inner resources. Along the way, you'll read real-life stories that illustrate the choices some of my clients made, and how they affected their leadership. I also invite you to look at your own leadership and personal requirements, and to consider the impact that taking care of your needs would have on strengthening your leadership mindset.

~ 3 ~

THE PURSUIT OF THE SOUL OF LEADERSHIP

Authentic leadership results from character, not status.

In the previous chapter, two business leaders spoke about striving to achieve leadership mastery or leadership excellence. This chapter describes the course of the road and the terrain we may encounter on this journey -- from departure to arrival. When we can anticipate what we might find along the way -- as well as the rewards that await us -- we can prepare for a more pleasant and powerful passage.

This journey focuses on a period of transition – a particular shift in life – and on it we learn to get in touch with the excellence within. It's a journey that progresses from the first stages of maturity – commonly known as adulthood – to *true maturity*, where we are in touch with our Wisdom. As we move along this road, we get to know the true Self and attain the generosity of spirit to stand on the leadership platform we looked at in Chapter 2.

During our individual as well as generational evolution, we go through Phases of Personal Development in which we move from viewing the world via our need to attend to Self to seeing it through our need to attend to others. This development continues in a spiral pattern, moving all the way from primal instinct for survival to, eventually, the highest level of consciousness known to man.

The road to the soul of leadership – the platform for leadership excellence where inspirational and authentic leadership abides – focuses on the stretch of the spiral where we cross from a place of *self-restriction and stagnation* to a place of *self-expansion and freedom*. This is a laborious and conscious transition in life that not everyone will choose to make, but in my view it is of *paramount* importance since it enables us to achieve not only leadership excellence and mastery, but also congruence and alignment as a person.

The reward of this difficult transition is the achievement of a state of true generosity of spirit; a state of genuine authenticity and self-acceptance, and, moreover, love for Self. From there, we can be of true service or help to others – absolutely and realistically – because we're already taking really good care of ourselves. Our values, our goals and our intentions are now in alignment. We have a healthy relationship with our ego, and it works with us and not against us.

From this perspective, and knowing what it takes to grow through this phase, we're in an excellent position to understand others without judging. We are able to assist our team, our peers, or our boss in their own development (if that's what they want), and to accept and see clearly where they are on their own growth path.

With this extended frame of reference we can have greater influence and develop our leadership platform. In leadership terms, and radically expressed, this refers to the transition from power-oriented management to authenticity in leadership. This is the journey to the *soul of leadership.*

THE PHASES OF PERSONAL DEVELOPMENT

There are several Phases of Personal Development. People whose awareness grows with the experiences presented by life will typically go through *the absorbent phase, the rebel phase,* and *the mirage phase,* commonly known as adulthood.

The absorbent phase and the rebel phase occur *prior* to maturity, while the mirage phase represents only the first stage of *true maturity,* and is based on knowledge. Although we all reach *physical* maturity as adults, not all of us mature *emotionally* to the same level. So in the mirage phase there's still a high percentage of ignorance that manifests in poor relationships, arrogance, a self-denying attitude, or stepping on others 'to get what *I* want'. I refer to this phase of development as the mirage because we are viewing a false reflection of life and what matters, however real it seems to us when we are there.

There are two further Phases of Personal Development – the *authenticity phase* and *the cosmic awareness phase* – but only a small percentage of people get to know these. When we arrive at the authenticity phase – where the soul of leadership dwells – we've found and trust our Wisdom, have attained true maturity and are in alignment with personal excellence. In this phase we've grown from emotional ignorance to emotional maturity, and we've gained an awareness of ourselves and our surroundings.

The greatest and the most inspiring business leaders of our time have developed a few steps beyond the point of authenticity to reach the *point of excellence*, where, while still relating to the material world, there's also a growing connection to life's purpose that generates an altruistic urge to give back and to serve.

This journey takes us from being inspired to being inspiring.

The final phase is cosmic awareness, where we have attained absolute maturity and feel a spiritual connection. Also founded in Wisdom, this phase is concerned with embracing emotional and *spiritual* maturity, and it's a state of being achieved by only a few. Leaders who develop to the cosmic awareness stage are likely to become disconnected from material matters and become concerned mainly with the spiritual and cosmic world. Their connection is with the Oneness.

We could speculate that people such as Gandhi, Mother Teresa, Einstein and the like would have approached the cosmic awareness phase, and Spiritual Masters and other enlightened spiritual figures have gone beyond this point. Because of the sense of disconnection from the mundane, leadership in this phase of *absolute maturity* and beyond ceases to be practical and becomes spiritual. And at that point it usually surpasses the stage of leadership excellence needed in the business and political worlds.

Let's now take a deeper look at the Phases of Personal Development. Please note that the stages given below are developmental phases, and are unrelated to age and physical growth. People achieve the phases at different ages, depending on their personal experiences, their attitude to life and their personal degree of open-mindedness or individual disposition to accept that which is different.

THE ABSORBENT PHASE

At the beginning of life a baby concentrates solely on its personal needs and is totally dependent on others for survival. The baby then becomes a child whose parameters are set by society, local customs and educators. He or she absorbs the paradigms, beliefs and values that are given, and within which he or she will live. The journey continues to the place where the child can take care of him- or herself.

THE REBEL PHASE

When we reach our teens the world takes on a different meaning. Our awareness of the emotional world expands and becomes mostly focused on 'me'. During the later teens comes the rebel phase – the stage of fighting against the values bestowed by others. In its simplest manifestation, there's only a questioning of such paradigms, although most people do not question, they just rebel for the sake of it, often propelled by the influence of peers or fashion. During this phase we tend to look at the world in terms of what the world can offer 'me' and we are easily convinced to protest against what does not cater for 'me'.

A small percentage of people stay in the rebel phase for life, acting like teenagers and being rebels without a cause. (I'm not talking here about situations of oppression, when 'rebellion' can be very conscious and 'for the greater good'.) However, most people eventually move from resisting to accepting again the old paradigms. Whether we alter the meaning and intensity of the old parameters depends on our willingness to open our minds to other views on life. The more open-minded we are, the faster and clearer we'll advance on the journey that takes us to the place commonly known as adulthood.

From this point we'll explore the arena concerned with the journey to the soul of leadership, so let's now take a look at the next two phases.

THE MIRAGE PHASE

In the mirage phase we take charge of becoming responsible and reliable adults who strive to get as good a job as possible, and our pursuit of success is reflected in our surroundings. Depending on how much we rebelled during the previous phase, we may or may not follow in the professional tradition of our family: in some cases for the love of such a vocation, and in others simply following the momentum generated by our elders.

In the mirage phase we are focused on the external world: we live according to *what we think the world expects from us.* In this illusory phase we live according to the rules of society – *we think what we're supposed to think* and *we are who we think we're supposed to be.* We're part of something innately familiar, and we behave like the people around us – within the boundaries of what's acceptable to the society we feel we belong to, or want to be accepted by.

In this phase appearances are very important, and we care very much what people think about us. We give ourselves identity according to others' perceptions, and we mirror what we think will help us belong – for example, buying an expensive car or designer clothes because they mean we've 'made it', or joining the most expensive golf or tennis club because of what they represent.

In this phase we don't question what we think or feel about the world. We're used to things being the way they are and need to feel a sense of 'belonging' with the people we know. We don't question *who* we are; we are just one of many. Therefore it comes naturally to compete to be the best in order to stand out, to feel admired, or to feel successful.

In striving for recognition and belonging, we don't question what we truly want because there's always someone else's approval to think about. *What will my children/parents/wife/ friends/husband/colleagues/society in general think about me if I...?* From this place it's easy to judge others, and we live in fear of how we ourselves might be judged. There's a strong and rigid view of right and wrong, and we can be very critical of anyone who is different; we might even feel threatened by them.

Getting Stuck in the Mirage Phase

Like insects caught in a spider's web, it's easy to get paralysed in the mirage phase due to our fears. Even if we think, deep down, *I have to sort this out; I have to move on to where I want to be,* it's very hard to make the move, or to change, because there are people we love, people we care about or those who have a hold on us, who want to keep us here. There's opposition to us embarking on the next part of the journey from those who feel threatened by us becoming more true to ourselves – by the fear of losing us. Therefore, we hold ourselves back, through the fear of loss, little realizing that we lose our Selves in the process.

In numerous societies this has been, and still is, a way of living. The vast majority of people *never* develop beyond the mirage phase and die without ever allowing their true Self to emerge. This is a phase of unconscious self-restriction in which it's easy to become stagnant. It becomes a web of constraint and potential entrapment. We find this type of life safe because this is what we know, but it's a mirage – an illusion.

The Departure Point

The mirage phase of restriction of Self is the comfort zone for the vast majority of us, since it provides a *false* sense of being in control of our lives. For those of us who have the longing for something else – like congruency, authenticity and great leadership – this comfort zone is not that comfortable. It's tiring to have to conform, and this type of life is rather empty; there is a void we need to fill. Deep down, we don't feel safe because we're mostly looking for approval from the wrong source. This is not the place of great leadership.

Recognizing that we want more out of life, and that we are the only ones who can make it happen, is the *departure point* on the journey to leadership excellence. Taking the first steps is frightening, and only a few pull away from such a strongly magnetized field of stagnation.

Pulling out of the mirage phase is worth every single second of the uncertainty it entails.

But the sometimes painful journey that follows is worth every second of the endurance it requires, since it brings the greatest reward of all – the sense of completion, together with a much stronger sense of belonging and ownership of Self. The reward is arriving home.

THE AUTHENTICITY PHASE

The aim of the journey to authenticity is to find self-alignment, congruence and inner peace, as well as freedom from constraint and the ability to live in accordance with our own rules. It's about knowing who we are and what we stand for, and being comfortable in our own skin. In other words, the aim is the achievement of personal acceptance and authenticity.

I refer to the authenticity phase as a place of personal excellence. Although it's probable that such a journey never ends, I speak about reaching the state where we truly accept ourselves; where the pain of transformation is over and the joy is full. This is a state of *true maturity*, where we live in accordance with our personal values, faithful and true to ourselves. It's a stage where genuine expression of Self is a way of life, and this level of excellence and authenticity is a state of personal, emotional, and, consequently, *professional* mellowness.

The road to authenticity leads to the *soul of leadership*: the platform, podium or ground for the Business Alchemist. Along the way we find the meaning of true generosity and service. In a beautiful paradox, the authenticity phase – which corresponds with the need to focus on the world of Self – is also the platform from where we can become midwives to others.

Authenticity is a state of being in which we *know ourselves*. We know our strengths and our shortcomings, and we can learn from them – because we're aware of our grey areas, we can choose to bring colour to them. When we achieve authenticity we have grown to be concerned with what *we, our selves*, think is right or wrong. In this place, duty and responsibility are self-determined.

In this place of *freedom*, we experience self-expansion and can be of true assistance to others because we know and accept ourselves. Although we're still driven to develop and improve, we're content with not being perfect because doing our best is good enough. We have stopped judging ourselves. We have arrived here after discovering who we truly are, and not only accepting but liking our Self.

A few steps ahead of reaching authenticity lies the ground for great leadership, because there's no fierce competition with colleagues. Instead, there's mutual respect, cooperation and generative alliances. When we live in this state of being we seem to be in the flow, and almost miraculously we seem to attract the people and the opportunities that are right for us. In this stage we act as a magnet for what will assist us in doing what's important for us to do for the world, as well as for our own fulfilment.

Along this road we discover that the more we know, the more there is still to learn. The further we walk, the further we want to go on and grow. And as we realize that we truly know very little, we find a place of humility that's real and genuine.

In the place of personal excellence, the only competition is with ourselves, because we know that we can deliver what others don't. The calibration is about finding the right cause, job, position or company that will allow us to carry on progressing, while giving us the opportunity to give back. On the platform of authentic leadership, we're already serving our life purpose, whether we know it consciously or not.

MAKING THE JOURNEY TO THE SOUL OF LEADERSHIP

As I mentioned above, it's difficult to start on this journey because there will be a lot of people pulling us back and wanting us to remain where we are for some reason or other.

On this journey there is loss: we lose beliefs that no longer work for us (although they might have done so in the past); we lose dreams that were not ours, and emotional debts that we made out of fear; and we lose some alliances and some relationships. We gradually let go of all that is pulling us back, both inside and outside of ourselves.

Loss can be very painful, but letting go is essential for growth. Imagine making a pilgrimage with a large, bulging suitcase. Too much baggage slows the pace and jeopardizes the journey. Eventually, it's necessary to lose some weight and probably replace the suitcase with a lighter rucksack.

The speed at which you advance on this journey, as on a pilgrimage, will be personal to you. There will be periods of time when you'll walk at the same pace as others, and spells when you'll be on your own. Sometimes your rest time will be spent alone, and sometimes you'll have company.

The growth on this journey happens in steps, and progress oscillates from one step to another. Some steps will take longer than others, and people you've left behind at one stage may be re-encountered further along the way.

Along this road there are no shortcuts: we must take *every* step. However, there are external factors that can accelerate our growth, propel us to question life, and help us to let go more quickly of some of the roles we've been playing. These influences can arrive in the form of a personal tragedy, a bereavement, an illness or an accident, or facing death – whether our own or that of someone close to us.

People who remain caught in the web of self-restriction will gradually be left behind and, although you might still choose to have contact with them, these relationships will no longer be gratifying. There's only so far we can advance while our feet remain tied, or when we feel weighed down by someone who doesn't contribute to our growth – either by pulling us back or by not supporting or encouraging us in our journey.

Halfway along this road we sever important ties. We either have a promotion or change the organization we work for, or we change career and profession. On a personal level, this is the stage when most divorces take place.

The good news is that, just as you sever some ties that impede you, you'll come across other people who'll bring much more to your life, your leadership and your growth. In business situations where several people take this journey at the same time, there can be mutual support and interchange – even when progress takes place at a different pace.

The road to authenticity and personal excellence is a journey of transformation that replaces layers of judgment, criticism and guilt with newfound force, self-knowing and acknowledgement of vulnerability. It's a transformation not to become someone else, but to bring your wonderful Self to the fore, allowing your true colours to shine through.

The soul of leadership is reached when leaders are truly themselves and trust their Wisdom; when they have achieved authenticity as a state of being. This is the leadership platform from which to generate Business Alchemy and become a catalyst for transformation. The path to personal growth enables leaders to offer their true best, while leading and developing others in the direction that will benefit the team, and the company, to mutual satisfaction and accomplishment. Excellent leadership generates transformation.

> *'I realized there had been a shift in my orientation to one of serving my team – by providing them with what they needed from me (which is not always the same as what they thought they wanted!) – and supporting their own growth as leaders, to serve their people in turn.'*
>
> **Stuart Fletcher, former president of Diageo, international division**

~ 4 ~

KNOW YOUR MIND AND MAKE IT YOUR ALLY

'Where attention goes, energy flows.'

Hawaiian Huna philosophy

We've all heard such expressions as *I've changed my mind, I'm in two minds about the matter, Make up your mind, That's a load off my mind,* and *It's all in the mind*. But these do bring a question: what do we mean by *the mind*? Is it thinking, or is it feeling? Or is it about both? Contrary to popular belief, the mind is concerned not only with thinking, but also with *feeling* – it encompasses both thought and emotion. Our minds contain the whole of our personal model of the world: the gauze through which we perceive our individual 'life' or chosen reality.

I have found time and again that some of the traits, qualities or parts of our personalities that have helped us to reach the current point in our lives become the very reason why we get stuck and stop progressing. The things that have been instrumental in driving us to accomplish the success or achievements we enjoy today are often instrumental in blocking further progress, preventing us from reaching the desired place or achievement of tomorrow.

In other words, what worked for us yesterday in bringing us to today is not necessarily what will work in taking us from today to tomorrow. If we're not progressing as we want to in any given area of our life, it's time to review our thinking. The energy, drive and strategy needed to arrive at a certain point are different from the energy, drive and strategy required to maintain or grow beyond such a point.

Let me explain how this works.

OUR INDIVIDUAL VERSION OF THE WORLD

Does your view of the world support you in being the best leader you can be? If you think about today, and about the obstacles you face – whether they're related to the economic climate or your relationship with your stockholders or your boss – do you have the mindset that best suits your desired style of leadership?

⚏ What initiates your action?

⚏ What drives you in your life?

⚏ What matters to you – *right now?*

⚏ And is it the same as what mattered yesterday?

Maybe you realize that you are repeating a certain pattern? If so, is it working? 'Today' is important, since today gives us an indication as to what's going on in our lives – what's working and what isn't.

The invisible force that drives us, and is the most powerful motor for action, is *emotion*. However great at planning or strategic thinking we may be, it's our emotions that propel us to act. If we were driven solely by thinking, perhaps we would do more things according to plan, and in our own interests. But sometimes we know intellectually what we need to do, yet we don't act on it. We often carry on obliviously, doing what we do – which is the perfect way to create a future that's just like our past.

It's easy to keep to our usual and familiar pattern; simply drifting along, leaving actions that concern important aspects of our lives for later. We often have other priorities, or we have no time, or we have too much work. We're likely to find many sound reasons not to act that aren't the major delaying factors at all. The real reason we delay something important is because we associate acting on it with an unwanted emotion that we'd prefer to avoid. We choose instead to stay in the comfort zone, in our 'drift'. The most common emotions that hold us back are fear, pain, guilt or boredom.

It's only when emotions strike that we experience our reality, and their force is enough to halt personal drive. We might associate these emotions with a past experience of unrewarded hard work, or fear of failure. Or perhaps we assume that we'll endure another similar experience if we take action. The greater the intensity of the emotions we feel, the greater the impact on the decision to act, or drift.

In order to break a pattern and create a different future, a shift in our individual version of the world is essential. The way we view the world sculpts our whole experience of life, since it shapes meaning and emotion, and therefore action. What's really needed to propel us forwards is the intensity of an empowering emotion, such as enthusiasm, joy, determination, anger, excitement, playfulness, curiosity or fun.

Intense association between action and unwanted emotion paralyses, while intense association with wanted emotion energizes. The greater the intensity of the emotion, the greater the drive to act or to stay put. If we bring in any empowering emotion with force, we can do anything.

Our individual version of the world is a filter; it shapes our way of being, our relationships with others, our priorities, our daily decision-making and, most importantly, the relationship we have with ourselves. It shapes our existence and how we participate within it.

Our version of the world is therefore our most precious possession, and we defend it and reinforce it with our actions. It's made up of our convictions – including our beliefs and our values – and it gives us a sense of identity. If anyone threatens our version of the world we feel as if our whole being is threatened, and we react accordingly.

How About a Karaoke Night?

Some of the convictions we hold about the world – about right and wrong, or about other people – evolve with life's mind-opening experiences. Other convictions, however, remain untouched, often because we don't even think about them.

For example, if we think about attending a karaoke night, it's very probable that we'll each have very different reactions to such an idea -- and that we'll have witnessed the different reactions of other people, too.

Some people enjoy karaoke, but others dread the very thought of it. Some enjoy it only if they've had a few drinks, and others are indifferent and can take it or leave it. For those with a strong dislike of the ridiculous, those who would not dare to sing in front of other people, or those who hate being the centre of attention, the whole idea of a karaoke night is simply dreadful. I've met people who want to disappear and spend the whole evening at the bar or in the toilet, hoping that no one will force them to get up on stage.

Then again, there are always the one or two who *love* getting the microphone, and whether they sing well or not, they just take part for the fun of it. Some people enjoy the attention; others believe that they sing well and take it very seriously, spending the whole night on stage while the rest of the audience wish they would get off it! And of course the 'take it or leave it' people might be completely indifferent: happy to sing or not. They can be good spectators -- having fun simply by watching others and participating from their seats.

All these reactions to the simple *thought* of the karaoke night respond to our diverse belief systems. The belief system we operate about how the world *is* or *should be,* is *unique to each of us.* However similar our belief system is to those of some other people, some of the time, the combination of beliefs that we hold, and the assumptions that we make about other people and about ourselves, are exclusive and particular to *every single one of us.*

HOW WE MAKE DECISIONS

The beliefs or assumptions that we hold are strongly attached to emotions, and can provoke a positive or negative emotional response. These beliefs or assumptions either support us and our goals and wellbeing, or hinder and limit us in our capacity for endurance and/or our choice of endeavour. We start building our belief system from the moment we feel emotion – so, from the minute we are born or, according to some theories, even earlier.

Two main factors contribute to this. Firstly, we take on our first set of beliefs and values in early childhood. They are given to us by our educators – such as parents or family – and are often imposed on us through the traits and customs of our country or region, the bestowed religion, school, or social status, according to the number of siblings and position in our family, and so on. In other words, our convictions are initially formed consciously by the culture in which we are raised. Culture gives us the first sense of *who we are.*

The second factor is our experience of life – based on our sensitivity to hurt and to joy. Because this process is driven by emotion, most of it is unconscious. As we grow up, we learn through observing, and by doing. We learn from our parents by copying what they do, and by being praised or criticized for our behaviour. We also learn through experience, such as discovering where the edges of the bed are by falling out of it, or getting an electric shock after putting our fingers in the wrong place. We have both physical and emotional memory, and we learn to associate hurt or pain, as well as joy or pleasure, with particular events.

Hurt and joy are our *only* motivators. Sometimes the avoidance of pain can be a stronger driver than the attraction of achieving joy or pleasure. Whenever we do anything, we attach an emotion to that action, and that determines whether we want to do it again, or not.

Experiences – to which we attach intensity of emotion – form the decisions that construct our belief system. Our beliefs support or limit us for action.

The Power of the Unconscious

Can you recall the first time that you rode a bike; the first time that you swam, or did anything significant? If, before we ever ride a bike, we see someone else fall off one and injure themselves, or we choose to believe the person who tells us that it's dangerous to ride a bike, then we might associate 'hurt' with the activity, even though we've experienced it only through our eyes or in our imagination.

On the other hand, if we've only ever seen people having a really good time riding a bike, we then associate the experience with joy, and it's likely that we'll want to 'have a go' and ride one ourselves. Our predisposition towards riding a bike in this case will be very different, because our emotional association is positive.

The fact is that we make a *decision* concerning the associated level of risk with an activity, and whether we want to accept or refuse this risk. Our decision is based on *perceived* as well as *factual* experience. Even a decision about something as simple as riding a bicycle could have an impact on our attitude to risk-taking later in life; the association with joy or hurt may be revealed again and extended to all kind of rides, thereby having a strong influence on our relationship with risk and the life choices we make.

We've all made many decisions like these, which are stored in the unconscious mind and rule our lives. We have made unconscious decisions over our capabilities, over our worth, over life's principles, over authority, over friendship, over the world... These decisions stick in our unconscious mind as beliefs, and they form our convictions. While some of them remain suitable and continue to enable and empower us, others, which may have served us as children, no longer work later on in life and become obstacles that hinder our progress.

Most of the judgments we make about ourselves are the result of unconscious decisions bound to a particular circumstance in early life where we experienced an emotion deeply enough to lead us to make that decision. Our self-opinion, and the role we take in life – whether we choose the role of the rescuer, the victim, the protector, the leader, the follower, the successful or the failure – are the result of the type of emotion we felt and the intensity with which we felt it.

> Here's something amazing about the mind:
> when we believe something very deeply,
> we adjust the evidence to suit our belief.

OVERCOMING OUR LIMITING BELIEFS

Beliefs that prevent us from being all that we want to be are 'limiting' or 'hindering' beliefs. Reviewing outdated convictions, and how they affect our lives, is paramount to our personal growth, both as leaders and as human beings.

As I mentioned earlier, the ability to build bridges is part of the essence of Alchemic leadership. All too often though, the assumptions that we make about other people, and what they 'should' be or do, stop us from reaching out to them. Bridges connect people to one another – they allow trust and recognition to develop between colleagues, and between leaders and their reports. As you will no doubt be aware, there are certain people with whom we feel an immediate connection, and there are others with whom we don't even want to make the effort.

However, if and when we do make that effort, and start building the bridge, sometimes our perception can change and we can develop an understanding that allows for an improved relationship. We don't need to *like* all those we work with, but developing a way to close the communication gap will prompt stronger communication and generate more effective results.

It's important to look at what lies within *us* that rejects a person ('He's an idiot'), their *behaviour* ('She interrupts all the time'), or *way of being* ('They just don't care'), and to recognize which of the assumptions we hold is contributing to our criticism of others. What belief or value are we holding on to that's not intrinsically ours and is keeping us in emotional ignorance? By opening our minds to a different outlook we can 'raise the bar' of our own perception and sharpen our emotional acuity.

Over the years I've come across many leaders with hindering convictions or limiting beliefs that prevented them from achieving their personal targets. Here's an example:

⌘ BUSINESS ALCHEMY IN ACTION ⌘

Sam was an extremely talented marketing director whose relationship with his company's sales director, Alex, was based on strong personal dislike. Although Sam recognized Alex's high professional values and excellent strategic aptitude, he also perceived him as a self-centred show-off and an arrogant bully who had complete disregard for other people's efforts, who didn't know how to behave with his colleagues, and who couldn't control his temper.

However many reasons Sam had to dislike Alex, it was absolutely necessary for the pair to develop a constructive and efficient professional relationship for the good of the business. Sam had to find a way to bypass Alex's tendency to throw regular tantrums. Even the *idea* of taking the first step in building a bridge towards Alex held great difficulty for Sam since, as he put it: 'Alex doesn't give a damn about others and cares only for himself.' This was Sam's clear assumption. He was convinced that Alex was 'being sneaky and inconsiderate' and this animosity was compounded by Sam's deeply held convictions that 'showing off is strongly in the *don't do* category', and that people who show off 'are too full of themselves'. Sam's beliefs were the biggest obstacle, not only to bridging the communication gap, but more importantly, to raising Sam's leadership to the next level.

During coaching Sam and I discussed the possibility that Alex's arrogance was simply a cover for personal insecurity and a fear of losing control. We worked together on considering how Alex might be viewing the world, and how that might be having an impact on his leadership and communication style.

Sam's immediate challenge was to find a way of speaking to Alex that was constructive and gained results. Many of their current exchanges were uncomfortable, and resulted in Sam feeling annoyed and demotivated. When this kind of pattern of non-communication becomes a habit, the way to change it is to find a new way of addressing one another.

Sam described Alex as being like a peacock continuously displaying his beautiful plumage, so we discussed the fact that the best way for Sam to deal with this was by acknowledging and paying attention to this need, therefore paying Alex a compliment. In that way Alex would feel appreciated; he'd be able to put his feathers away and get on with daily business.

Sam was sceptical, but he approached Alex openly and put on the table the transparent intention of building a cooperative and respect-based relationship with him – one in which they could learn from each other for the sake of improved results and the organization.

Alex's response was unexpected. He recognized that he had difficulty in controlling his tantrums and really wanted to change. He readily agreed to lunches with Sam to achieve more understanding and alignment between their respective departments. By acknowledging some vulnerability, accepting his shortcomings and cooperating with Sam's proposal, Alex made it easier for the pair to begin to make their professional relationship stronger.

Building Bridges

The coaching process included some illuminating 'Aha' moments for Sam. He realized that he'd been holding the hindering conviction that *you need to be it, not show it*, and therefore condemned 'showing off' as *bad*. This belief was now replaced by a more empowering conviction: 'If I want the world to know my strengths, I have to be ready to show what I'm made of sometimes through my achievements.'

Acknowledging his hindering convictions was vital in order for Sam to change the following:

- His original conviction that talking to Alex would be a waste of time.

- The assumption that Alex didn't care.

The empowering convictions he adopted as a result were:

- 'I can and I will influence relationships with my input.'

- 'Transparency and clarifying early assumptions will bring better relationships.'

- 'Some people's need for recognition will lead them to show off. I can use that as a sign to give them reassurance if I consider it appropriate.'

By building a bridge, it became possible for Sam to find a way of dealing with Alex, and in doing so, open doors to other possibilities, awaken resources and become more emotionally detached from judgment, criticism and the power of other people's emotions.

RECOGNIZING YOUR OWN REALITY

We've explored the amazing way that the mind works, so now let me guide you into discovering it for yourself. I'm going to appeal to your sense of curiosity, and trust you'll make the most of this simple and quick exercise. If you wish, you can download it at www.pilargodino.com

In order to maximize your fun and enjoyment of the exercise, play along with me for a few minutes so that you get to experience it fully. It's important that you follow the steps as I ask you to, or you could spoil the outcome.

EXERCISE: EXPLORING YOUR STYLE

~~~

First, choose a pleasant memory from your past. Once you've selected one, close your eyes and go fully into the memory; enjoy it for however long you find it pleasurable. (Average time 30–60 seconds). When you've finished, come back to the book and continue to the next step.

Pause for 30–60 seconds.

Now take a moment to rate the intensity of the experience on a scale of 1 to 10. Make a mental or physical note of your rating. (It doesn't matter how you measure it, as long as you use the same measuring system throughout the exercise.)

Next, think about some events you would want to happen *in the future*, and choose one you really desire. Once you've selected the event you want, relax, and with your eyes closed, imagine that you are in the moment this is going to happen. Immerse yourself in the moment and enjoy it with all your senses – see what you'd see, hear what you'd hear, and feel what you'd feel if you were in this desired moment. Again, stay there for as long as you enjoy it. (Around one minute.) Then continue to the next step.

Pause for a few seconds.

Now that you are back, take a moment again to rate the intensity of this experience, using the same system as before.

Now compare the intensity ratings of your first and second imaginary ventures. Which had the highest score – the memory of the past event or your imagined future event?

~~~

Interpreting Your Results

I've done this exercise with more than 1,000 people. Below is a breakdown of their results so you can compare them to your own.

Intensity Higher on the Past Memory: 33 Per Cent

Your mind finds it easier to attach emotion to events in the past than to future plans or events. You find that past experience is your basis for doing things. You consider yourself realistic and factual, and you might find yourself reminiscing about the good old days. The downside is that you might dread a certain type of occurrence because of how you felt about it in the past, and you might find change challenging.

Intensity Equal on Past Memory and Imagined Future: 27 Per Cent

Your mind finds it as easy to attach emotion to past events as to future plans and events. It's very interesting to know that the mind does not differentiate between so-called real and imaginary experiences. You count within your strengths the ability to apply your past experience towards making your desired future. It's possible that you added to your memory bank some experiences that only happened in your daydreams, or that happened to someone else, but you added enough emotion to make them a reality. Therefore, you could find yourself wondering whether something you imagined very strongly really did happen or not. You are gifted with the ability to enjoy the present moment.

Intensity Higher on the Imagined Future: 40 Per Cent

You find it easy to attach emotion to future events, plans and goals. This is the preference I've found in most leaders, and it's the most helpful scenario for bringing on the passion necessary to attain and achieve. The downside is that you're likely to live in the future, and that could occasionally bring on some anxiety. You'll benefit from remembering to enjoy the moment, and giving yourself a small (or large) celebration each time you achieve something.

If you're thinking that every person who does this exercise will draw the same conclusion as you, I invite you to make this your next party trick. You'll find that the spread is fairly even. Within the diverse results of this small exercise, we can acknowledge what many experts on the workings of the mind have explained over the centuries as different views of 'reality'. The mind does not differentiate between the lived or the imagined event. As long as there's an emotional attachment to it, both are acknowledged as real. The higher the intensity of the emotion attached, the stronger the experience of reality.

Lastly, here's another example of a leader who identified and then overcame his limiting beliefs:

⌁ BUSINESS ALCHEMY IN ACTION ⌁

Through my leadership journey I came to know that what I was doing well naturally I could amplify by doing it intentionally. I also found that things I thought I was doing well were getting stagnant, and I needed new tools and a change of mindset to turn them into potent assets. My biggest awakening was to see that recognizing a restricting belief is a trigger to change, and improve not only personal performance, but life itself.

Initially I was too proud to recognize that I was holding on to entrenched beliefs about my view of the world with the same intensity of passion that I applied to my work. This led me to hold the greatest restricting belief of all – that it was going to be difficult to change my beliefs, or even to work on them. Noticing that the restricting beliefs I held about myself were even stronger than those I held about others, and about business situations, was powerful. However, working on my own restrictions was much more transformative.

The most intense beliefs I held were as follows: 'My experience and leadership position allows me to do tasks better and faster than other people.' This belief restricted my capacity for delegating – hence I was not so good at a basic leadership task. I now recognize that, while I'm a good leader and do tasks fast and well, there are others who are as fast, or better than me, although they may not have the same level of experience.

Then came: 'I'm faster than others, and therefore I am cleverer than them.' Well, fast and clever are definitely not the same thing, and on occasion speed interferes with cleverness.

The next belief was: 'I have a greater level of self-assurance and confidence than others and that's why they respect me.' While it's true that I'm self-assured and confident – both respectful qualities – I discovered that many people respect me for my capacity to roll up my sleeves and work with them, for my enthusiasm and my 'Let's do it' approach. I'm most respected for my ability to engage people, and help them believe in what we do. Self-assurance and confidence are the vehicles to inspire the same self-assurance and confidence in others.

Lastly, there was: 'I'm very demanding on quality and others don't care as much.' I realized that perfectionism is not my exclusive domain, and it's not always the best modus operandi. Getting very bogged down in quality issues can mean losing sight of other important factors in the equation.

~ 5 ~

CHOOSING PRIORITIES: KNOWING WHAT YOU REALLY WANT

The most important question we can ask ourselves is this: 'What's important to me: what's truly important to me in each area of my life?' Within the answer to this question lives the very heart of self-motivation. Getting to the essence of what we deeply want exposes the unconscious elements that influence our decisions, and reveals the *criteria* for what we do and the keys to prioritizing.

FINDING YOUR CRITERIA: CHOOSING YOUR PRIORITIES

These criteria are to motivation and behaviour what the trunk is to a tree. Criteria are the sturdy foundations that support and influence other factors, such as decision-making and choosing one thing over another.

We elicit our criteria in two stages. Firstly we ask the question 'What's important to me?' and secondly we *rank* the criteria that we identify in answering this question. The two exercises that follow will take you through these stages.

EXERCISE: HOW TO FIND YOUR CRITERIA

~~~

To discover the potency of the concept of identifying criteria, I encourage you to write down everything that crosses your mind when you ask yourself the questions below, since you might want to return to your responses as you read parts 3 and 4 of the book.

This exercise will help you to understand the factors that influence your motivation, and ensure that the choices you make in life are aligned with *who you really are*.

- What's important to me in my work?
- What makes me want to go to work?
- What would put me off wanting to go to work?
- What's important to me in life?
- What's important to me in a relationship?
- What do I need from the other party?
- What's important for me as a parent? As a son or daughter? As a friend?
- What keeps me going?
- What turns me off?
- What's important to me in my leisure time, at the golf club, on holiday, etc?

~~~

Knowing what draws us *towards* something – recognizing the elements that make us say 'yes' – means that we can make choices that are congruent with who we are. Once we are conscious of our wants and needs, we place ourselves in the position to get them – and to say 'no' to any distraction. Understanding our longing illuminates the choices we've made in the past, and ensures a clearer path towards the future.

If we say 'yes' to work, to relationships, to opportunities, to anything that's not aligned to our criteria, we'll eventually lose interest.

RANKING YOUR CRITERIA

I thought I knew what was important to me: harmony, friends, good relationships, fun, solving problems, people, achieving, a good job, physical activity, excitement, enthusiasm... However, when I questioned myself more deeply, I found that learning and sharing, and interesting conversations, were at the core of most of those elements – together with good vibes, of course. Today I know that almost everything I enjoy involves these deeper criteria.

Next, I ranked all these elements in order of importance. I noticed, much to my surprise and self-judgment, that although I had expected 'harmony', 'achievement' and 'relationships' to be at the top, what I truly search for is interesting, intelligent conversation first, and then the rest. When I realized this, I understood my past career and relationship trajectory, and I immediately saw my future very differently. So, if you wanted to offer me a job, you'd need to ensure that the opportunity to exercise my top criteria was on offer; then I'd say 'yes'. If interesting communication is not there, my answer will be 'no'.

Once you understand what drives your motivation, and its effect on your behaviour and commitment to endeavours, you'll understand the influence you can have on people around you – as long as you know and respect what *they* want. Therefore, if you want to engage someone at your place of work, or reach agreement in a business proposition, but you offer it according solely to *your own* criteria, you might meet resistance. However, if you make the offer to include *their* criteria too, they will say 'yes'. This is the basis of win-win relationships.

Lack of awareness of one's own criteria is often embedded in self-doubt and frustration, even depression. You'll observe this in the case of one former client who I will call Zack in order to respect confidentiality. As I tell Zack's story, you might find certain things obvious, which he, at that moment, was not able to see despite his high intelligence. After all, 'we all have blind spots that become obvious when finally revealed'.

~ BUSINESS ALCHEMY IN ACTION ~

Always successful, and able to make a very good living, Zack had hit a low point and was on the border of depression. He'd lost his job due to lack of motivation and was cracking under the pressure of keeping everybody thinking all was 'business as usual'. He didn't dare tell anyone that he'd lost his job. He felt he was a failure and didn't want others to know – initially because he thought he'd find another job soon enough, and later because the snowball was rolling.

Zack told me how, in every job he'd ever had, he'd lost motivation, and so he kept on changing companies. He was aware that this was not the way forward. He held the common convictions that 'once you are in a good director role, you stay and enjoy your success', and 'when you are in the fortunate position to be making enough money to give your family a good life, it's your responsibility to carry on doing that'.

Zack felt a failure because he thought he'd lost motivation due to pressure. This turned out to be true, but his pressure was not due to the pressure of the *job*, but to the pressure of living his life according to someone else's criteria.

The fact is that Zack wanted the best for his family. Of course he wanted to give them the best that money could buy, but when he got bored with his job, he carried on solely because of what his father, father-in-law, wife and everyone else would think of him, whether his assumptions were real or not.

When we worked through the exercise above he identified that his necessary criteria for work were 'a challenge', a 'sense of achievement', the 'feeling that I add value', 'organizing', 'pushing for change', and 'gaining results'. Zack was excellent at turning around the performance of companies that were in jeopardy, and he really enjoyed bringing them back to profit. He would introduce procedures to get everything running smoothly, but at that point his enthusiasm would fade and he'd lose motivation. So, every 18 months to two years, he'd had enough and he would leave.

For a time Zack went into a very deep financial and personal crisis because he didn't really understand what was going wrong. He told himself that he should be happy with work, and that there was something wrong with him because he couldn't hold a job down; that he was a failure. He was seriously hard on himself and blamed himself for the precarious situation his family was now in. His self-judgment was blinding him and he couldn't see a way out.

Reaching the realization of what he truly wanted was enormously liberating for Zack. What he enjoyed was the process of turning companies around from crisis mode to a position of profit and growth. He was motivated by the challenge of the task – by solving difficulties and by the process of change – but he found the ongoing maintenance of the result very boring.

By knowing his criteria, he recognized his core strengths. Instead of criticizing himself for wanting to change job every few years, he began to recognize the advantages of such a pattern. He finally turned what he regarded as his failure (the 'two year itch'), into his biggest asset. The moment he appreciated what he wanted out of life, and what he wanted out of his job, was the moment he realized he could be happy in his work and achieve success *his way.*

Zack has since worked successfully as a crisis manager for different companies. He has made the most of his longing and now puts his passion into what he enjoys most. He works at a higher rate of pay for a shorter working period while he turns things round, leaving the ongoing maintenance of the results to someone else.

In learning to understand his own criteria, Zack learned to ask and elicit other people's criteria as well. He now uses this skill to delegate the right task to the right person; to motivate his teams and to maintain motivation himself.

Have You Found Your Criteria?

Now you can relate to the importance of criteria, and ranking it, take a moment to think about your emotional reaction to Zack's story. Taking into account what the story has awakened in you, let's revisit Stage 1 and think again about *what's really important to you.*

- ⚏ What do I want at work?
- ⚏ What demotivates me?
- ⚏ What would my ideal day at work encompass?
- ⚏ Am I compromising anything vital?

Now let's explore deeper by asking:

- What would I gain when I get... (your criterion)?
- Where does this lead me?
- What do I ultimately want to obtain?

EXERCISE: HOW TO RANK YOUR CRITERIA

The process of ranking will reveal your *core criteria*.

Begin by comparing one criterion with each of the others in sequence, until you have created a hierarchy. Here are some examples to get you started.

In my case I began by asking myself, 'What's more important to me: achievement or harmony?'

Of course I want both, but is one contained in the other, or are they separate qualities? I considered which would be more vital to me in a job, life, sport... The answer matters only to me, since my idea of achievement is unique.

Next I chose to consider whether work achievement is more important to me than harmony. I continued by comparing 'achievement' with 'fun'. I decided that when I achieve I have fun, so I chose 'achievement' as my priority again. Then I compared 'achievement' and 'intelligent conversation' and I chose 'intelligent conversation'.

At this point intelligent conversation became my top criterion. I then compared my number one to the rest, then number two with the rest, and so on until I had established my order.

Since criteria usually comprise only a few elements – often between three and seven depending on the individual – it's relatively easy and quick to get your own ranking.

~~~

Knowing your criteria can help you to decide between one job or company and another, one opportunity or another, one relationship or another. It sharpens your ability to prioritize, and it's the basis of persuasion. Eliciting the criteria of the people you want to influence will give you the key to motivate and engage them; the key to getting their commitment.

IDENTIFYING OTHERS' CRITERIA

In my opinion, the best way to get to know the criteria of another person, or of a group – whether at work or in private life – is simply to ask. When we elicit others' criteria we don't need to rank them in order to influence, the general criteria will be enough. At work with your team, you can use the yearly appraisal meeting to ask *'What's important to you?'*

They will like you more for it and they will know you care. I suggest you start asking everyone this question, because it's good practice. You'll be surprised by both the answers and the reactions you get. This is the first question to ask when implementing Business Alchemy. It's the key to earning people's commitment and trust, and the permission to serve and develop your team.

Respect people's criteria, because they are attached to identity and values.

Criteria define what is particularly meaningful to each of us as individuals. They are the words we use to express our values, which vary within different contexts. If we want to influence people it's helpful to know what's important for them. In order to know this we can listen actively and/or we can also ask them the following questions:

- ◢ 'What do you want in… ?' (context)
- ◢ 'What's important to you in… ?' (context)

In order to maximize the chances for influence, and get a positive response, we can repeat the words the person uses in order to obtain and maintain their attention. They connect each of these words with emotions, so they are very powerful.

Here one of my clients highlights the benefits of identifying criteria:

⟶ BUSINESS ALCHEMY IN ACTION ⟵

I wanted to increase my personal efficiency as a sales manager, and the efficiency of my sales team. Business Alchemy gave me new insight, and helped me to change perspective and find awareness of my own strengths and weaknesses. As a result, the knowledge of my own resources improved, and with it my performance as a leader.

I gained a fresh understanding of my needs and the team's needs, and consequently my relationship with them went from strength to strength. I found myself using the 'language of influence' and communicating more effectively with the team, which has led to increased sales, greater performance and stronger staff retention.

PART 3

THE LANGUAGE
OF INFLUENCE
AND THE LENSES

'In this ambiguous world, nothing is false, nothing is true. All depends on the colour of the lens we see it through.'

Ramón de Campoamor, 16th-century Spanish poet

~ INTRODUCTION ~

Have you ever passionately defended an opinion during an argument – totally convinced of the absolute truth – only to think later that perhaps the other person had a point? Even, sometimes, to the extreme where you saw things very differently from how you'd regarded them earlier? We all like to be right.

In fact, in any discussion we have, at the time we *are* right. This is due to the *lenses* we look through to see the world. When we're in an 'I'm right' mood, we can see only through our own eyes. Later we might see things differently simply because, in a different context, we look through a different lens.

Think about someone you *want* to influence: it could be your boss or a direct report, a peer, or someone in your personal life. Now think about a time when you *were* having influence on them: when you had a really good grip on the situation. Then recall a time when you did not have an influence on them. If you haven't yet influenced this particular person, then think about a time when you influenced someone else. What's important here is to compare the two situations so that you identify your *key influencing factors*.

What was different in the two situations? Was it the circumstances, or was it the context? Was it the other person's mood, or was it yours?

INTRODUCING THE LENSES

The lenses we choose to use in any given context provoke behaviour that eventually becomes a pattern. We continuously give away information through the language we use – not only in our choice of words, but also in our body language. If we listen with intention, we'll notice that people reveal what motivates them – how they think, how they make decisions – in any particular context.

Each of the lenses covered in this section of the book represents a frame of reference – a filter through which we perceive the world. They define our thought processes and influence how we express ourselves, and how we see and evaluate. They shape our likes and dislikes, who/what we find it easy to relate to, and who/what we find challenging.

There are no right or wrong lenses. Lenses are not fixed; they vary according to context and circumstances. They can be altered consciously and used to explore, and eventually accept, different viewpoints. They can expand your mindset.

In the explanation and methodology that follow, I talk about the different lenses, how they work, and how to use the *language* of each lens. To master such a powerful and influential mindset, you might want to try on each of the lenses, and to experience them as much as possible as you read along in order to:

- recognize your own lenses; reflect on what you see, what you say, what you do, and what invites you to act.

- recognize other people's lenses; think about what those around you say and do, and what incites them to act. This will help you recognize which lenses they use, and in which context.

Once you can recognize how the lenses function, and which lenses are being used at certain times, you'll be in a position to anticipate and influence behaviour – both in yourself and in those around you.

Knowledge of how the lenses work is an effective leadership tool:

- to help place the right person in the right job, in task allocation.

- to engage, motivate and appreciate variety among the team.

- to extract the best from each individual and advance their development.

- to encourage people to adapt to change, embrace the unfamiliar and grow in confidence.

The lenses can be used to discover something new about yourself, to know and understand others, and as a process of Alchemy, both for you and for your team.

Guidelines for Using the Lenses

When calibrating the lenses, it's of paramount importance that you stick to one context at a time. For instance, if you work as a director, it's important that you look at your lenses in the context of your role, since it's likely that in a context other than work, and in other trivial matters, you'll use a different set of lenses.

I've seen numerous clients use the lenses unconsciously in ways and contexts that have limited them and caused them significant personal or relational discomfort. I want you to have conscious access to the lenses that will benefit you the most, and to be able to choose those you wish to use in any particular area of your life.

If you find you're using lenses that are no longer serving you, you can change them by reflecting on your unconscious decisions and limiting beliefs (see Chapter 4 for an explanation of how these develop).

I highlight and underline that no given lens is either 'good' or 'bad' outside a specific context and desired outcome. The lenses are also not a form of personality typing. Even though I sometimes describe a lens 'type', I mean this only in the context of work. That is, a person may use one lens in one context, and a different lens in another.

At the end of every chapter in this section of the book, I include a set of words and a style of language that can be used to influence each of the lenses.

~ 6 ~

PERSONAL PERSPECTIVE:
THE PICTURE/DETAIL LENS

This lens determines the 'portion size' of information we handle best: whether we favour overviews, summaries and bottom lines, or whether we prefer detail in order to understand something, to express ourselves and to feel understood.

The lens in this chapter facilitates the language for you to communicate with intention and obtain a positive response.

IDENTIFYING PERSONAL PERSPECTIVE

Do you know someone who, in normal conversation, tends to give you too much information? Sometimes even to the point where you feel irritated, want to run away, or beg them to stop? (Or maybe all of these things?)

And do you also know someone who usually leaves you wanting to know more?

As a leader you're likely to feel comfortable with the whole picture, as well as zooming in and out from the picture to the detail as and when required.

Take a moment now to consider your world scope:

- Do you tend to see things first in terms of the whole picture or the detail?

- What tends to be your priority for attention – the broad view, the small print, or somewhere in between?

- Do you find it easy to keep your eye on the goal? Or do you get bogged down by the daily oiling of the machine?

- Are you where you want to be? Or would it be useful to move your attention a little?

- Do you need to know everything that's going on in order to feel in control?

- How well do you delegate?

Those who prefer the broad Picture lens are likely to feel constrained or irritated during conversations about dotting every 'i' and crossing each and every 't'. Those who use the Picture lens find that too much detail obscures understanding and detracts from clarity, making communication and prioritization almost impossible.

Those using the Detail lens handle small pieces of information well, but at the extreme, they cannot create or perceive an overview. Detail people need detail in order to understand; they talk about every aspect because it's essential to their need to be understood. They need to know that the details have been taken care of before considering taking a step towards a broader view.

The first thing to be aware of is that it's easier to zoom from Picture into Detail, than for someone using a Detail lens to jump up to a helicopter view.

THROUGH THE PICTURE LENS

It's likely that, as a leader, you prefer to be given a summary or a list of bullet points and then decide to drill deeper as necessary.

But it's of vital importance to understand the difficulty experienced by a Detail person when asked to give a summary, or think in bullet points. Those who insist on giving you all the information possible – dates, amounts, statistics and so on – will only feel content when they have taken every contingency into account, and looked at everything in what can seem like painful depth. They need to know that you, as the person they're speaking to, have taken full account of all their finer points of concern.

Have you ever spoken with someone and been convinced that they knew what you were talking about when in fact they didn't? I sometimes think that I've shared a chain of thought that I haven't. I continue talking from my point of thought, but since people don't live in my head they cannot follow me. When we are in Picture lens mode we may generalize to the point of omitting information that others need in order to know what on Earth we're talking about. We forget that they don't live inside our head. We may just give a series of bullet points that don't give them the full picture.

THROUGH THE DETAIL LENS

If the Detail lens person's view is disregarded, they can feel dismissed, and there's a chance they will take it personally, viewing the lack of interest from the person using the Picture lens as a lack of respect. It's essential for the Detail lens person to also recognize that offering too much attention to detail will cause those viewing through a Picture lens to lose interest and switch off, want to physically climb the walls, or scream, depending on their preference.

As a leader you'll be the judge of when to use this information for the best. If you want to fully engage a Detail-oriented person in achieving your vision – and for them to make your vision their own – you'll need to show recognition for the importance of what they do. It's essential for them to be acknowledged and appreciated. If you want to persuade a Detail person to welcome the view through your Picture lens, they need to know you'll take account of what's important to them.

As a leader you need to ensure that the Detail person knows that you understand how important their approach is to the success of the project, as well as acknowledging that you do not process extensive detail as readily as they do. In this way, they are valued as an active member of the team.

LEARNING TO RESPECT AND APPRECIATE DIFFERENCES

How do people who use a Picture lens at work typically view those who are Detail-focused?

NEGATIVES	POSITIVES
They slow things down.	I can trust them with accuracy.
They block progress.	I know they'll give me all the information I need.
They can't prioritize.	They have the knowledge at their fingertips.
They get bogged down in the detail.	I know they'll have thought of everything.

How do those who use a Detail lens at work typically view those who are Picture-focused?

NEGATIVES	POSITIVES
They don't think about everything we do.	They are visionaries.
They are abrupt, and sometimes rude.	They are courageous.
They aren't realistic.	They are motivators.
They don't understand what's involved.	They are great at prioritizing.
They spend all their time in meetings.	They are great at decision-making.

Both the Picture and the Detail views are necessary for success: the dynamics of the dance between the two will determine the pace of progress, and whether a positive and complete outcome is achieved. The two extremes complement one another.

SEEING THE WORLD THROUGH THE PICTURE/DETAIL LENS

What would happen to the Picture without the Detail?

It would remain a dream.

What would happen to the Detail if there were no Picture?

It would remain a static collection of unrelated details. It would be meaningless.

However, basic misunderstandings between those whose preferences are at opposite ends of the spectrum can trigger a great deal of negativity, emotion and discomfort – potentially causing discord and undermining teamwork.

Leaders have a greater responsibility to learn to value colleagues, and to see the world from others' perspective as well as their own. It's important for us all to know that we have differences, and to learn to respect and embrace them.

As already discussed, both the Picture and the Detail perspectives are essential for success – the bottom line is that any team needs both. However, the Picture people will always want to have a helicopter view and zoom in and out, whereas the Detail people may remain focused on the importance of having all the information to hand. By learning to see the world from each other's point of view, and in exploring their view in their language, a greater understanding can be achieved.

EXERCISE: IDENTIFY THE LENS BY LISTENING TO WHAT PEOPLE SAY OR DO

Picture: Give an overview; talk in bullet points; give a single sentence; go straight to the point; can handle detail only for short periods of time.

Detail: Talk a lot, giving plenty of detail; can go off at a tangent; can make a mountain out of a molehill.

What to say to get a response:

Picture: Give a summary or bullet points. Trust that they will ask if they want to know more. Use words and phrases such as: 'generally', 'essentially', 'so the bottom line is...', 'in a nutshell'.

Detail: To make this lens comfortable, it's necessary to go into a little more detail, repeating key words that are important to them. Use words and phrases that denote detail, such us: 'exactly', 'specifically', 'precisely', 'give some detail'.

In a Nutshell

The Picture succeeds through the implemented Detail. The Detail gains meaning and purpose only within the framework of a Picture.

~ 7 ~

REALIZE DUTY ORIENTATION: THE PEOPLE/TASK LENS

Consider the following scenario. A leader wants to set up an awayday for his team of 130 people. It's to be organized by the 'awayday group', which is made up of four out-of-hours volunteers, two of whom are his direct reports and two of whom are HR volunteers.

IDENTIFYING REALIZE DUTY ORIENTATION

If *you* were in charge of this task, what would you do as a first step?

⌐ Would you develop a time span and assign tasks straight away? Or would you think about who would prefer doing what and accommodate their needs?

If the pressure was on and the project was delayed, how would you react?

⌐ Would you get tough on the group to make sure they deliver? Or go easy on them since you understand they are busy and after all, this is an extra task?

Are you placing people's feelings and needs *before* the task? Or are you setting and enforcing schedules and paying attention to the task *first*? Perhaps you are catering for people and focusing on the task, taking both equally into account?

In a work context, the majority of people are Task-oriented and simply want to get things done. A minority are totally People-oriented – focused entirely on making people their priority, wanting them to be content and trying to accommodate their needs. Around a third of employees are a combination of the two.

THROUGH THE PEOPLE/TASK LENS

People-oriented and Task-oriented traits are both important within an organization; however, very few posts will be suitable for a purely People-oriented person. By their very nature, most roles require a fine sense of task. Departments such as human resources, recruitment, customer services and so on may attract People-oriented staff, but the majority will still need to be able to deliver to plan and on schedule. Those who are totally People-oriented are motivated more by simply being in the company of others than by the task in hand.

Task-oriented employees are generally best suited to departments such as Information and Communication Technology, manufacturing, production, operations and so on, where their attention to results is put to best effect. Task-oriented people can be helpful, warm and engaging, though the task and results remain their priority. It's a good idea to pay attention to matching the right type of lens-person to the role, or to address the development of their relevant lens preference, in order to achieve and maintain optimum output and wellbeing.

You can decide what the optimum position in this lens would be for you in your present position. By understanding what your natural tendencies are, you can either choose the type of company/department that suits your preference, or work on developing the lens tendency needed for your existing position.

Understanding Context

Let me make it clear that Task-oriented individuals *do care* about people. They feel as much as any People-oriented person, but they simply view people as an intrinsic part of the task. For instance, when Task-oriented people come to visit, they leave just as they arrived. They get up, they say their goodbyes, and they go. Of course they visit because they want to see you, but their focus is on the visit (the 'task'); they will rarely outstay their welcome.

People-oriented individuals do care about tasks, although often the people *become* their task. When they come to visit, their focus is on you; they will stay with you as long as there is rapport. On leaving, they will keep you at the door for a long time and will find it difficult to break the contact. They tend to take things personally.

In personal relationships, this lens difference becomes apparent in conversations where one of the partners is concerned about having their feelings taken into account and wants to talk about what the other part feels, while the other partner is focused more on closing the issue and moving on. Both partners will feel deeply, but only one will want to linger on the feelings; the other will be matter-of-fact and take it from there.

LEARNING TO RESPECT AND APPRECIATE DIFFERENCES

How do People-oriented people typically view those who are Task-focused?

NEGATIVES	POSITIVES
They are difficult to work with.	They get the job done.
They don't care for people.	They don't waste time.
They are workaholics.	They take care of quality.
They don't have a life outside work.	They work long hours.
They are terrible communicators.	They get results.

How do Task-focused people typically view those who are People-oriented?

NEGATIVES	POSITIVES
They are too concerned about people's feelings.	They know who is who, and what's going on.
They are touchy-feely and take things personally.	They cut slack for others.
They spend too much time 'chatting by the coffee machine'.	They are approachable and interested in other people.

SEEING THE WORLD THROUGH THE PEOPLE/TASK LENS

What would happen if everyone made 'People' the main priority?

All energy would go into keeping people happy; commercial concerns would be given secondary focus. In an extreme situation, results would be terrible, and business activity would come to a halt.

What would happen if everyone made 'Tasks' the main priority?

There would be an impersonal and cold atmosphere in the workplace; a lack of regard for personal circumstances; likelihood of nervous breakdown; the needs of staff would not be protected and nurtured; staff would become demotivated and turnover would be high.

EXERCISE: IDENTIFY THE LENS BY LISTENING TO WHAT PEOPLE SAY OR DO

~~~

People: Talk about feelings; make feelings and concerns the task.

Task: Focus on task, things, systems, ideas, tools; getting the job done is their priority.

What to say to get a response:

People: Use the person's name; explain what people like; acknowledge feelings (using the word 'feelings' is enough). Say 'it feels…'.

Task: Talk about things, systems, process, goals. Say 'Let's do…'

~~~

In a Nutshell

Modern organizations recognize the importance of becoming more People-oriented and endeavour to find the balance between ensuring the business not only survives but blossoms, while also looking after their people.

Here, one of my clients, a Financial Director, explains how he found a practical balance between People and Task:

⮞ BUSINESS ALCHEMY IN ACTION ⮜

I've always been the nice guy, but through the process of Business Alchemy, I became aware of certain obstacles I was putting in my own way. I've always believed that I'm an excellent relationship builder, but my awakening moment was to realize I held the hidden belief that to be firm, hard, or engage in 'difficult' conversations would break a good relationship, or make me appear disrespectful.

This hidden belief stopped me from doing all those things so necessary for my leadership role, and now I see clearly that the belief was crap! It's precisely because good relationships are based on trust, respect and understanding that I have not only the right but also the duty to be clear and firm in my communication, and to allow the other party to hear what I have to say.

I now live with the supporting belief that, by being transparent, authentic and honest, I can build strong and long-lasting relationships; this truly makes me an excellent relationship builder. Also, it's possible to build a strong and effective professional relationship while holding opposite views of the world.

It was also important to realize that trying to be an understanding and 'nice' person was leading me to support my colleagues and peers to such an extent that I took on tasks that belonged to them, in order to help. I now operate from the belief that the best help I can provide consists of a little guidance and support, and to let them do the task themselves.

PART 4

USING THE LENSES TO INFLUENCE AND MOTIVATE YOUR TEAM

All motivation is self-motivation — we cannot motivate others, we can only trigger or activate their own motivation.

∽ INTRODUCTION ∽

Before we look at the lenses of motivation, allow me to address a few points.

We do not and cannot motivate people – any more than we can change them – we can only trigger their motivation mechanism. The universal motivational triggers are *Recognition* and *Belonging*. We had a look at this concept in Chapter 1 when we looked at inspiring leadership. When we're in the company of someone who brings out the best in us, we feel important – they make us feel that we belong because they give us *recognition*. This motivates us to become even better and get more of it.

Feeling important is *the one and only* longing of the seven billion people on the planet. How we arrive at that feeling, and how long it lasts, will depend on us. If we like what we do and the people we do it with, and have the opportunity to bring ourselves, and our resources, to what we do, we will maintain momentum and motivation.

It's easy to assume that people already know what we think about them and their performance, but some people need to hear and also to see evidence of appreciation. It's up to us to provide this evidence and maintain motivation through our own leadership style.

As a leader you can spark your team's motivation by giving recognition, and creating a workplace where people want to belong, making sure that each person knows how important they are for you, for the team and for the achievement of the goals.

~ 8 ~

DIRECTION OF MOVEMENT: THE TOWARDS/AWAY FROM LENS

This lens is key in today's business world, where the pressure is high and people suffer from stress or burnout.

In my work as a leadership coach I find repeatedly that my clients don't have the time they need to listen to the problems their reports bring to them. Their line managers don't want to hear about what's not working, unless there are also suggestions and solutions for how to put things right. This is due to their Motivation Direction, as observed in this lens.

The Towards/Away From lens applies not only to people but also to organizations. In my experience, this makes it one of the most vital lenses to understand, in all its complexity.

IDENTIFYING DIRECTION OF MOVEMENT

There are only two factors to be considered when motivating people, and these are *Pleasure* and *Pain*. The Towards/Away

From lens relates to movement *towards* pleasure or *away from* pain. It's the old story of the carrot and the stick: we are either driven towards something because we want it, or motivated to move away from something that we don't want.

Most successful leaders use the Towards lens because they are goal-oriented; they are motivated to achieve, to get results, to attain, and they focus on priorities. They may show an element of Away From thinking to avoid obstacles, but their main motivation to get through anything is to keep an eye on the goal.

Think about the kinds of things that motivate you to take action:

- Are you driven by your desire to succeed, and the results?

- Is your greater motivation your fear of anything unwanted if you don't take action?

- Does the desire to achieve your goals motivate you towards work?

- Or are you driven more by the awareness that you may lose something if you don't keep striving?

THROUGH THE TOWARDS/AWAY FROM LENS

Those who use a Towards lens move ahead towards their goal. Those who use an Away From lens are motivated by the immediate need to fix things or people – by troubleshooting, or simply by escaping an unwanted situation, whether that's pressure, a deadline or the threat of failure.

There are also those who start Away From something and then turn Towards a goal. The results of a 1990s study by Rodger Bailey (described in *Words That Change Minds* by Shelley Rose Chavet, 1997) using a 'motivation test' showed that 40 per cent of people in a work context were motivated Towards, and the same percentage of people were motivated Away From. Still in the work context, a further 20 per cent of people were a combination of both traits.

The important thing is to become aware of your personal tendency and preference – especially within the work context.

Understanding Context

Remember that *all* the lenses are contextual. It's more than possible for people who are Towards-oriented at work to use an Away From lens when forming close relationships, or in personal finances (or vice versa). Some people who start out as Away From may transform their approach to a committed Towards attitude once their concerns have been addressed. Once they have *begun* to move away from that which they do not want, *they will not stop* until they have reached the place where they feel safe. Then they can relate to the goal as being the thing that will take them even further away from their initial concerns.

Similarly, a committed Towards person may come to a grinding halt if they encounter obstacles they hadn't anticipated, and have to sort things out before resuming their idea or project. After that, they may or may not decide to use an Away From lens in that particular context for a period of time, and learn through experience.

LISTENING TO LANGUAGE

It's easy to tell whether people are naturally Towards or Away From, simply by listening to the way they describe actions and opportunities. Ask a Towards person why they are going on holiday and they may tell you that the location is wonderful, with amazing history and architecture, that the nightlife is exciting and the food is meant to be delicious.

Ask an Away From person the same question and they'll tell you that they're going in order to get away from work, that they're bored with the poor weather at home, or that their golf club is closing for refurbishment.

You are hearing two different responses. One person is telling you, 'I want to go', while the other is saying, 'I need to get away'. You can find out someone's natural preference by asking everyday questions, and you'll also hear it in regular conversation.

Some other questions to ask in order to identify the lens are:

⌐ 'What will having "X" do for you?'

⌐ 'What's the point of this?'

⌐ 'What's in it for you?'

USING THE LENS TO MOTIVATE YOUR TEAM

The Towards/Away From lens relates to our relationship with risk. In my experience, the majority of leaders tend to use a Towards lens at work. They are often pioneers or trailblazers.

The Towards lens motivates leaders to take, or even incite, risks in order to achieve the goal.

The downside is, because we tend to measure others by our own yardstick, Towards-oriented leaders may assume that every individual in their team will be motivated in the same way that they are. They become very enthusiastic, energetic and 'full on' about their wonderful new project, only to generate scepticism and disbelief in 40 per cent of their organization. So, when addressing your whole team at once, it's important to deliver a combination of Towards and Away From language if you want to *motivate* people and make sure you *don't lose* their enthusiasm.

The best way for leaders to motivate everyone in the team is to cater for the natural direction of their motivation: encouraging the Towards-oriented to obtain a goal and stating or threatening the Away Froms with the unwanted situation.

There's a natural tendency for Towards people to assume that if they want someone to follow their lead, it makes sense to share their plans and enthusiasm, so they'll come along. This approach works well with people using the same lens: these are definitely the people who'll want to get straight to the goal! Towards people enjoy working with other Towards people because they are goal-motivated and enthusiastic, and therefore spark motivation.

However, a different approach is needed when leading Away From people. Too much Towards-style language will have the opposite effect and demotivate an Away From person. It will remind them of all the things that can go wrong and have not been considered. The more Towards the language, the more Away Froms will question, and the further away they'll move. If you want to motivate an Away From person, it's essential to align your style of talking to reflect Away From thinking.

Away From people will move Towards the goal only when the fear of getting what they *don't want* becomes greater than their concerns about moving. They need to know that all their worries have been taken into account before they'll even consider listening. Crisis management is associated mainly with an Away From motivation pattern, followed by motivation to move Towards the final goal.

When motivating someone who is in Towards mode, it's important to direct them straight *towards* something – in other words, be careful not to deliver too many comments in an Away From style, because you'll lose their attention. There's nothing more demotivating for a Towards person with a great idea than immediately hearing about everything that can go wrong. Their response is likely to be irritation, impatience and wanting to get on with it.

The danger for any Away From person working in a Towards organization is that if they do not learn to speak Towards language, they may be branded as negative, and in the extreme, could be overlooked for promotion, especially if they report to a purely Towards-style leader.

One of the greatest errors that leaders can make at work is to insist on trying to motivate Away From-oriented people in a Towards manner.

I've found this also to be the case in leaders I've coached who use an Away From lens, but adopt a Towards lens within an extremely Towards-style organization. This type of lens starts in an Away From place and then moves into a Towards pattern.

While this type of person is probably the most successful of the three tendencies – in their capacity to cater equally for both the obstacles and the goal – they find themselves in trouble because they *start* by talking about what can go wrong and *then* move on to the different possibilities for achieving the goal.

Their best strategy is either to keep quiet until their Towards pattern kicks in, or alternatively to change their initial approach and translate it into the language of the organization in order to attain the appropriate rewards.

Robert Dilts, the world-renowned NLP developer, has done extensive research into the arena of Towards/Away From. One of the fascinating things he found is that some US entrepreneurs who become millionaires more than once are mainly Away From in their approach to wealth; whereas those who are motivated by wealth creation for its own sake tend to be Towards in their attitude. Those who are Away From are motivated more by the desire to move Away From poverty. They are driven by the need to ensure that poverty is a state they never go back to.

LEARNING TO RESPECT AND APPRECIATE DIFFERENCES

Typically, a Towards person is quite frustrated by an Away From attitude, and may find team members discouraging, hard to motivate, uncooperative and stubborn. Likewise, extremely Away From people may literally stay *away from* Towards people because they find their approach foolish and unbearable.

As a leader you might want to encourage each team member to think about the positive traits their colleagues bring to the table, and help them to develop an understanding of why they might react in certain ways when under pressure. Away From people are usually brilliant at quality control and are excellent troubleshooters, while Towards people are very good at getting on with things.

How do people who use a Towards lens at work typically view those who are Away From?

NEGATIVES	POSITIVES
They focus on negatives instead of positives.	They are very good at finding errors.
They deflate enthusiasm by voicing doubts.	They anticipate what can go wrong.
They may put others under pressure.	Their best work is often produced under pressure.
They lack initial momentum.	They are good at short deadlines.
They can't be bothered.	They have very clear 'no go' areas.
They can't focus on the goal for long.	They are great firefighters.

How do people who use an Away From lens at work typically view those who are Towards?

NEGATIVES	POSITIVES
They are impulsive and foolish.	They have the passion to work around obstacles.
They are fast-paced and demanding.	They are very focused.
They are blindly optimistic.	They always see possibilities.
They are pushy.	They are decisive and highly enthusiastic.
They are too naïve.	They maintain positive momentum.

SEEING THE WORLD THROUGH THE TOWARDS/ AWAY FROM LENS

What would happen if everyone were Towards in their approach?

There would be no precautions, and no plan B. When obstacles arose, things would be worked through, or they would work around the hindrance; the goal would remain the only focus. There would be a waste of energy, effort, time and resources.

In the worst-case scenario there would be a realization – too late – that the goal is unattainable, after spending great resources (financial and human), as well as time and effort. It would be one of those projects that goes terribly wrong.

What would happen if everyone were Away From in their approach?

There would be troubleshooting, immediate firefighting and short-term problem-solving; also a tendency to go round in circles without attaining major goals. Undue priority would be given to a thorough approach to avoid problems. There would be many distractions and no route to the long-term goal. Priorities would be lost.

Working together ensures possible threats are considered before moving forward in a thorough and assertive manner, leading to a greater chance of success and a quality result.

EXERCISE: IDENTIFY THE LENS BY LISTENING TO WHAT PEOPLE SAY OR DO

~~~

Towards: Talk about what they want, about achieving, moving towards a goal, overcoming obstacles, delegating, staying focused; they prefer large goals.

Away From: Talk about what they don't want; will move away from strain, prepare the ground, hang on to control, get distracted; they prefer short deadlines.

What to say to get a response:

Towards: Use words and phrases such as: 'obtain', 'achieve', 'have', 'I want X', 'gain', 'getting things done'.

Away From: Say 'get rid of', 'leave behind', 'I do not want Y', 'not to lose', 'avoiding mistakes'.

~~~

In a Nutshell

Towards people keep their eye on the target, have clear priorities and have tremendous passion to work through obstacles.

Away From people suggest precautionary measures to ensure that all that can go wrong is taken care of, and if possible, avoided.

~ 9 ~

MOTIVES FOR ACTION: THE OPTIONS/PROCEDURES LENS

The Options/Procedures lens is concerned with understanding why we choose what we choose. Is it because it brings us possibilities, or because it gives us a method?

IDENTIFYING MOTIVES FOR ACTION

My friend Nigel is a brilliant cook. I've enjoyed eating his food and watching him work; he cares about what he cooks and how he cooks it. First he gets the kitchen ready, and then he opens his recipe book and follows each step of the recipe to the letter. Every meal is perfect every time; he is unerringly reliable.

On one occasion, when one of the ingredients had gone off and had to be thrown away, Nigel went through a considerable amount of stress. All my suggestions about equivalents or alternatives were in vain: he only breathed easily when I finally agreed to go out and buy the key ingredient. The prospect of substituting anything else caused him great concern and strain. The meal was a success, as always.

This incident made me think about how differently I behave in the kitchen. Although I too care about what I cook, my idea of fun is experimenting with food. Even when I attempt to cook something twice the same way, it's simply not possible since I view recipes more as a guideline for playing with food than as a rule for cooking. Even the salads I prepare are rarely the same.

If Nigel is cooking, I can anticipate a predictably good meal, with the same beautiful flavours of the time before. When I prepare food the meals are sometimes my average tasty food, but at other times they can be deliciously original and full of flavour.

So, in the context of cooking, Nigel needs to follow method, whereas I prefer to play with the possibilities. He's using a Procedures lens and I'm using an Options lens.

Take a moment now to consider *your* preference:

- Are you attracted to the opportunities and possibilities of doing things in different ways? Or do you like to follow a 'recipe' for success?

- Do you tend to follow the rules? Or can you not help but break them sometimes?

- Do you start things, follow them through, and finish them – all in consequent order? If so, does that come naturally to you, or does it require effort?

- Do you prefer several choices before you make a decision? Or would you prefer less choice and more method so you can 'just get on with it'?

⇌ If you've ever been in an IKEA store, do you follow comfortably the route you are supposed to follow? Or does it drive you mad and propel you to try to locate shortcuts to find your way to the freedom of the warehouse?

THROUGH THE OPTIONS/PROCEDURES LENS

The world of Options is the world of possibilities: the mind is opened to all the things we can or cannot do. However, in order to do any of these things, we need to start, follow and finish the task.

The world of Procedures is the world of finishing what we start: following the structure of a beginning, a middle and an end.

Those Using the Options Lens at Work:

⇌ Explore different possibilities to achieve a result, or different ways to avoid something.

⇌ Are interested in *what* to do, and in choice.

⇌ Create procedures to get from A to B and/or C and/or D... but will have difficulty following them.

⇌ Are excellent at bringing different views to the table.

⇌ Are interested in starting things, and may be attracted to another option halfway through.

⇌ Will do things in different ways in search of what works best.

⇌ Need to see or explore the alternatives in order to make decisions.

⇌ Are bound to break or bend the rules (even their own).

Those Using the Procedures Lens at Work:

⇌ Believe there's a *right* way to do things.

⇌ Are interested in *how* to do things.

⇌ Are good at following a method from beginning to end.

⇌ Feel confused if too many options are brought to the table.

⇌ Feel comfortable following the same procedure again and again.

⇌ Are compelled to finish things.

⇌ Will not welcome a change of plan after a decision has been made.

⇌ Are comfortable following instructions.

To achieve anything with a sense of order and control, we generally follow a process. Even the most Options-oriented person will have to follow some kind of Procedure when it comes to getting things done.

The differences between the Options/Procedures lenses are easy to spot. Once you're attuned to the differences in mindset you'll notice Options/Procedures discussions going on around you – in every family, at every airport and in every supermarket aisle – as well as in the business environment.

LISTENING TO LANGUAGE

If we talk to an Options person solely with the language of Procedures they will switch off, and vice versa. Options language tends to be open-ended and alert to new opportunities, whereas Procedures language tends to be more about how to proceed. There are clear advantages to both approaches, depending on role and function.

OPTIONS LANGUAGE	PROCEDURES LANGUAGE
What are the options?	How do you want it?
We have several choices.	It has to be done like this.
We need to remain flexible.	We need to remain on track.
We could do X, B, Z or J.	First we do X, then Y and finally Z.
Anything could happen.	The plan is ...first, followed by... and then...
Variety is the spice of life.	Each thing in its place.
There may be last-minute changes.	There will be no changes.
We could extend if necessary.	We will finish at...
I will play it by ear.	I will follow the script.
When we go to B we could visit X	We're going to B; X is another trip.
I like to vary my route to work.	I prefer to take the same route to work.

Every business needs to incorporate some form of procedure into its work structure in order to be successful, and those who tend to resist procedures, by nature and preference, will inevitably try to stretch the boundaries of procedures in order to gain flexibility. The irony is that it's frequently the business leader – the one who instigated the need for the procedure in the first place – who wants the system to be flexible enough to deliver well and on time, but also to be able to accommodate new ideas and fast changes.

If you read the instructions below carefully, you'll notice the use of language that each lens type will feel inclined to want to understand.

Options Language

There are several possibilities for an Options person to influence a Procedures person to consider different opportunities, as long as they involve a method with clear steps to lead them there.

Procedures Language

The only way for a Procedures person to have influence over an Options person is to give them choice. As the leader of someone who has great difficulty in seeing alternatives, you have the option to create a procedure to lead them to those alternatives.

USING THE LENS TO MOTIVATE YOUR TEAM

Someone whose role it is to monitor quality control will be using a Detail, Away From and Procedures lens at work, but may well use a Picture, Towards and Options lens at home: happy to opt, on impulse, for a weekend in a dream location… or two.

Similarly, the leader who is Towards and Options by nature is still likely to have an acute capacity for Detail or Procedures when necessary – especially in relation to achieving their goal – such as paying attention to the small print of an agreement, or when designing and implementing a method to deliver and follow up successful results.

Whether you are working in an Option- or Procedure-oriented department or organization, there will be times when options narrow and procedures must reign. To use a metaphor: when the sea is calm the sailors can choose when and whether to take their shift, enjoy the view of the moon, feel the breeze or smell the sea air. However, when the breeze becomes a storm, the sailors will go to their posts and follow the emergency procedures already established, responding only to the order of the captain.

LEARNING TO RESPECT AND APPRECIATE DIFFERENCES

How do people who use an Options lens at work typically view those who are Procedures?

NEGATIVES	POSITIVES
They are boring.	They are totally reliable.
There's no flexibility.	They produce results, even under pressure.
The pace is rigid.	They understand the requirements.
There's a lack of creativity.	They finish things.
There's too much bureaucracy.	They seem to know where they are.

How do people who use a Procedures lens at work typically view those who are Options?

NEGATIVES	POSITIVES
They are frustrating to work with.	They are creative in their approach.
They are easily distracted.	They explore new (and better) ways of doing things.
They cause disruption.	They are open to progressive changes.
They don't always deliver.	They want what's best for the product or company.
They lack clarity and can cause confusion.	They see different possibilities.
They delay schedules.	They make decisions based on different data.

SEEING THE WORLD THROUGH THE OPTIONS/ PROCEDURE LENS

What would happen if everyone were Options in their approach?

There would be continuous brainstorming and not much would be accomplished. There would be a lot of thinking about different choices, many things started, too much exploration and no execution. Rules would be made but not followed: the rule would be 'bend the rules'.

What would happen if everyone were Procedures in their approach?

The only way of doing things would be the 'right' way: the approach would be rigid. There would be no attention paid to improving things, and the rule would be 'If it works, let's keep it like this.'

In order to achieve goals, we need to successfully combine both an Options and a Procedures approach by choosing the option that's the most appropriate or beneficial and eventually selecting a method to follow through to the end. Where there's an intrinsic lack of respect, or antagonism, between these viewpoints, the productivity and quality of the organization will be under threat.

Check what happens in your own company: have a look in your organization at the Options/Procedures relationship within sales, finance, marketing, IT, HR and so on.

EXERCISE: IDENTIFY THE LENS BY LISTENING TO WHAT PEOPLE SAY OR DO

Options: Get motivated by possibilities, choices, alternatives and opportunities. Get distracted by other options; are bound to act against the rules; always want to do things differently.

Procedures: Get energized by methods and techniques. They are compelled to finish what is started.

What to say to get a response:

Options: Use words and phrases such as 'choice', 'alternative', 'we'll break the rules', 'just for you', 'we'll make an exception', 'possibilities'.

Procedures: Say 'the right way'; 'first, second...'; 'all tried and tested'; 'reliable'; 'methodical'.

~~~

In a Nutshell

A combination of Options and Procedures mindsets, plus mutual respect and embracing each other's strengths, are 'musts' for any organization wishing to become strong, innovative and productive.

~ 10 ~

TAKING ACTION: THE DOING/ASSESSING LENS

This lens looks at whether we're inclined to take the initiative, or whether we tend to let others act before we do.

IDENTIFYING TAKING ACTION

What's your initial reaction when you read the quote below from Karren Brady, a very active English businesswoman – she's a sporting executive (a former managing director of Birmingham City Football Club and current vice-chairman of West Ham United), a television broadcaster and a newspaper columnist.

> 'In the world there are people who make things happen, people who watch things happen, and the ones who wonder what happened.'

As a leader you're likely to have placed yourself in the first category. I've heard Karren use this quote several times, and on every occasion it provokes laughter. My guess is that the laughter comes from all those people who *make things happen,* and use the Doing lens at work. I would also add another category to Karren's assessment: 'the people who help things happen', which is implicit within the 'making things happen' and refers to those who use the Assessing lens.

THROUGH THE DOING LENS

Often referred to as proactive, Doing people initiate. They jump into action without much reflection and they're quick to respond. They usually speak quickly, and use short, direct, crisp and clear sentences that transmit the message, 'I'm in charge of my world and I create my own luck.' They go for what they want without immediately considering the consequences, and without much planning. They assess as they go along. They can be pushy. And at the extreme, they upset others because they are oblivious to people's boundaries when trying to get the job done.

THROUGH THE ASSESSING LENS

People who use the Assessing lens are often referred to as reactive, or thinkers. They first like to assess what they're going to do, often allowing others to get into action first. They feel nervous about starting any endeavour, because they need to know the situation is right before acting; therefore, they prefer to wait and analyse their response.

They are great analysts, and are good at considering all possible consequences – they also take other people's boundaries into account. At the extreme, though, they upset others by thinking too much about doing, while never getting to the point of action. They use passive language: describing actions that are a response to something outside of themselves. They transmit the message, 'What I do responds to some kind of need', or 'Life happens *to* me.'

> It's essential for those using the Doing lens — especially leaders — to realize that Assessing lens people also collaborate and participate, only at a slower pace and in a responsive fashion. They are 'the people who help things happen'.

LISTENING TO LANGUAGE

The Doing/Assessing lens is not so much about language as about movement; you will recognize the trait through the *speed* of the action.

DOING LANGUAGE	ASSESSING LANGUAGE
I organize meetings.	Some people question the need for meetings, but it's important for people to feel listened to.
I do, I act, I initiate, I'm in control.	I respond; I'm thinking about doing…

USING THE LENS TO MOTIVATE YOUR TEAM

If you operate as a Doing person, you generally want others to be more like you. Doing people prefer everyone to be fast and proactive. It's natural for business leaders – many of whom have that mindset by nature – to want to be surrounded by those who are similar in attitude to themselves.

However, when leading an extremely Doing person you need to steer the direction of action and the pace, or they'll act independently and may be in danger of following the wrong track, realizing their error only when it's too late. (The Doing lens in combination with the Options lens at work will mean that they'll start a thousand things and finish none of them.)

Assessing people, on the other hand, tend to excel at following up and finishing what a Doing lens person starts. They prefer to stay clear of extremely proactive people because they make them feel uneasy. Assessing people are often judged harshly in the workplace because they are less likely to instigate action quickly, and they may sometimes be considered a handicap because of their more cautious attitude.

However, they bring core strengths to the team. They are not go-getters and respond slowly but surely, and once they're ready and the situation is right, they get on with the task until the end. People who combine an Assessing approach with a Procedures lens are often the ones who get the job finished, and on time.

Raising awareness of the strengths of both traits will lead to greater understanding and cooperation among colleagues.

LEARNING TO RESPECT AND APPRECIATE DIFFERENCES

How do people who use a Doing lens at work typically view those who are Assessing?

NEGATIVES	POSITIVES
They think too much and do too little.	They are good thinkers.
They are too slow, and in the worst case, they are lazy.	They don't get in the way.
They need to get their act together.	I can get them to finish things for me.

How do Assessing people typically view those who are Doing?

NEGATIVES	POSITIVES
They act before they think.	They are enthusiastic, brave, clever, fast...
They want everyone to be like them.	They are highly motivated to start things.
They can be pushy and invasive.	
They stop at nothing to get what they want.	

SEEING THE WORLD THROUGH THE DOING/ ASSESSING LENS

Proactivity is a trait that's recognized and sought after by companies. Job advertisements often state that 'a proactive person is wanted...'. However, that's not always what the company *truly* wants or needs; it depends on the role. While it's true that being proactive and using the Doing lens is a trait of successful people, the Doing approach needs to be combined with a process-oriented lens such as Procedures, or there's a danger that the candidate will be good at beginning tasks, but not finishing them.

What would happen if everyone were Doing in their approach?

Tasks would be started before the full instructions had been given. All things would be started. You'd only see the dust left after the take-off. Many tasks would be unfinished.

What would happen if everyone were Assessing in their approach?

There would be lots of analysing action and much thinking about doing, but not much done. Tasks would only be done as a *reaction* to a need. The process would be slow.

A Curious Fact about 'The Stages of Action'

The drive that's needed to start something is very different from the type of energy that's required to maintain momentum, and different again from the stamina that's needed to finish things. That's three different types of energy – all of which are needed in order to achieve a successful outcome.

Each of us is able to produce all three types of energy when working on solo projects, although one type of energy is more natural for us and we have to make an effort to bring out the others.

As a guideline, the lenses that respond to each stage of action are:

Starting: Towards, Doing

Maintaining: good balance between Doing and Assessing

Finishing: Procedures, Assessing.

For long and complex tasks, it's essential to build a team of people who together encompass all three types of energy – and between them use all the lenses – so that the desired outcome is achieved without too much wear. If everyone on the team were to prefer *Doing*, lots of things would get started, but the amount of effort necessary for finishing could prove too much – depending on the length of the endeavour and the combination of lenses.

Doing/Options lens-users tend to keep falling in love with the next task at hand: they may be in the midst of one task and then, halfway through, decide to jump to another one because the fun element is completed and they want some more fun elsewhere.

It's important to be aware that wherever you place yourself on the Doing/Assessing continuum, it takes effort and emotional energy to deal with the person who is at the other extreme. The reality of the matter is that both sides have pros and cons.

EXERCISE: IDENTIFY THE LENS BY LISTENING TO WHAT PEOPLE SAY OR DO

~~~

Doing: Use short sentences, active verbs, action words.

Assessing: Say 'I might consider it when the time is right', or 'I'm thinking about going, doing, joining...'. They use incomplete sentences.

What to say to get a response:

Doing: Say 'Do it', 'Go for it', 'Let's do it', 'This is the time', 'now'.

Assessing: Say 'consider', 'wait until', 'understand', 'think about', 'might', 'could', 'would'.

~~~

In a Nutshell

Doing people are driven to start tasks. Assessing people are driven to continue and finish those tasks.

PART 5

THE BUSINESS ALCHEMIST AT WORK

'People are always blaming their
circumstances for what they are.
I don't believe in circumstances.
The people who get on in this world
are the people who get up and look
for the circumstances they want, and,
if they can't find them, make them.'
George Bernard Shaw

⤳ INTRODUCTION ⤶

To get up and look for the circumstances we want, and make them happen, we first need to know what we truly want, and what circumstances are best suited to achieve it. For that, we need to reflect and search for what's working well, what's missing and what we have in excess.

This section of the book adjusts its rhythm to become a practical guide for applying the knowledge acquired so far to the realities of day-to-day business. Chapter 11 looks at self-feedback and taking time to recognize the most common impediments to excellent and Alchemic leadership, based on the experience and stories of other leaders.

Chapter 12 takes a Procedure-oriented approach for successful implementation, offering you direction and guidelines for creating a new, more personal method of influencing, monitoring, and giving feedback to your teams.

Parts 1 to 4 of the book focused on the nature of Alchemic leadership, and invited you to use different lenses to see the world from the point of view of others. As we've seen, effective and influential conversations with direct or functional reports are developed and enhanced when we understand how they think, recognize why they do what they do, and acknowledge their natural preferences for thinking and behaving. This is even more imperative and significant in a multicultural environment.

When we use the lenses as tools, with the conscious intention of relating to another's world as much as possible – paying attention to how they express themselves – we are in fact listening to what they *mean*, not only to what they *say*. This is the most advanced type of active listening.

So far we have looked at:

- Business Alchemy as an approach to achieving results while developing people and improving performance.

- Discovering something new about you and your leadership style.

- Reflecting on your needs and the needs of others.

- Increasing understanding of team members: their motivation and behaviour.

- Practising conversations that influence, with the aid of the different lenses.

- The value of active listening.

Now that you have a greater perception and understanding of people's daily attitudes, you're ready to achieve great success by putting Business Alchemy into practice.

In Part 5 we look at:

⚎ Our energy management and listening to our needs.

⚎ The habits that challenge our leadership.

⚎ Our commitment to our Selves.

⚎ Applying techniques and action steps for effective feedback.

⚎ Using the Alchemic approach to achieve results, while developing people and improving performance.

⚎ Practical examples and personal stories for opening the mind to new ways of action.

～ 11 ～

SELF-FEEDBACK:
TIME TO THINK

'The definition of insanity is doing the same thing over
and over again and expecting different results.'

Albert Einstein

We all know the above quote by Einstein to be true, and yet
it's so easy to get caught in the trap of thinking and doing in a
manner we've made our habit.

In this chapter we look at the main self-inflicted traps
or situations that I've found drive leaders to exhaustion,
demotivation, extreme frustration, and, in some cases, close to
depression. To raise new questions we need to give ourselves
time to think – to allow the imagination to find new angles and
to reflect – so that we can recognize our limits, accept them
and move beyond them.

KNOWING YOUR WANTS AND NEEDS

The key characteristics of high-performing leaders and
successful teams are *perspective, clarity* and *self-awareness*.

The most successful leaders are self-reflective. They take time for themselves, stepping back to think about their performance, their shortcomings and strengths, their present and their future, their wants and their needs.

Knowing our needs is the first step to achieving great performance and fulfilment. Even if we think our needs are already being met in one field – whether professional, emotional, personal or spiritual – we could find greater enjoyment and accomplish more still if we were to meet them in as many fields as possible.

For instance, more and more people turn to their work to fulfil their need to feel valued, and this distracts from making the effort to meet the same level of need in other aspects of life. However, if we *were* to meet our needs in all domains, we would, without doubt, become stronger professionals and stronger leaders. We would start to build the inner support necessary to feel at the top of our game.

There are two main areas to look at – your wants and your needs.

Looking at Your Wants

Ask yourself:

- If I could have anything I want, what would it be?
- If I were to dare to think big, with no limitations and no obstacles, what would I really want?

Looking at Your Needs

Ask yourself:

- ⌐ 'What do I need to do in order to achieve or accomplish the above wants?'

This question refers more to strategy, but you can also search further, by asking:

- ⌐ What are my mental, emotional, physical and spiritual needs? What's important for me to be content and to know I'm on the right track?'

Knowing your wants and needs will also assist you in confirming whether you are in the right job, post or organization.

THE HAMSTER WHEEL

Lack of self-enquiry leads us to slowly create a vicious circle for ourselves in which we persist unconsciously in our endeavours, oblivious to what's going on inside us. Like a hamster on its wheel, we do the same things over and over again, taking on whatever comes our way and not stopping to think about the personal consequences of the load.

High pressure, crazy agendas and impossible schedules are the norm for today's leaders. The overwhelming mountain of deadlines, obstacles, a massive workload and difficulty in meeting targets increases dissatisfaction and brings a lack of perspective. In such circumstances it's common to react in two main ways: directing the frustration towards others in *Explosion,* or directing the emotion towards ourselves in *Implosion.*

When pressure is high and their team doesn't seem to be as efficient as they would like it to be, some leaders become critical and focus only on the shortcomings of those around them. In the team, this brings out a sense of not being regarded as competent, and in the leader a sense that the team cannot be relied upon, thus demotivating the led as well as the leader.

Some leaders react to pressure by taking it on their own shoulders, increasing their work hours steadily until they're doing the work of two or more people. By the time I find them, they have lowered self-esteem, and great doubts about their capabilities as leaders.

> **It seems a strong paradox, but it's only when we attend to our own needs that we're able to give of our best to others and the world.**

In other words, it's easy to lose sight of what's truly important for us. Even leaders who are motivated by pressure and love a challenge have a limit, which is easily overlooked. When the limit is crossed, it leads, inevitably, to exhaustion, and anything requires great effort. When the excessive pressure of daily demands takes over there's a tendency to let frustration and/or tiredness rule, thus camouflaging the original enthusiasm and enjoyment of what made them choose the job in the first place.

So let me ask you this:

✍ 'How are you? Truly, how are you?'

If we first discount the invalid answers – 'Fine', 'Not too bad', 'OK', 'All right' – then what is your answer?

Matter-of-fact leaders address the overload by replying, 'This is what there is and I just get on with it.' However, in the course of coaching many leaders I've found that beneath the impulse to dismiss the answer, most of them are very tired; in fact, many are nearing exhaustion. They don't even allow themselves time to consider how they really are, being too involved in the day-to-day, fearing the consequences, or simply carrying on in a vicious circle, like the hamster on the wheel.

It's not only logical but essential to develop your leadership role and take it as far as you want to; it's also vital to grow with the role you hold, and to become more and more the leader you want to be.

My questions would be:

- 'Are you growing into your role? Or has the growth turned into a struggle?'

- 'Do you feel free to be yourself? Or is the pressure such that you feel forced into "what to do" and "what not to do"?'

- 'How much are you moulding your role to you, and how much is your role moulding you?'

- 'Is the hamster wheel blinding you to your need to give time to yourself?'

⇌ BUSINESS ALCHEMY IN ACTION ⇌

One senior executive, who'd recently returned to work after sick leave, decided that he had to prove he deserved to retain his position. With that objective, he took work home at night and at weekends, working altogether longer and harder than he'd worked before his illness.

Over time he developed a strong sense of guilt. He'd think about the work he had to do while spending time with his children, and then he thought about the small amount of time and attention he gave his children while working at home. He created a pattern of forgetting to *be in the present* in whatever he was doing.

Through coaching he decided to give himself permission to think and pursue what *he* wanted – to take time to receive training, to immerse himself fully in his endeavours, giving 100 per cent attention to whatever he focuses on. He's now enjoying his work again, and is working altogether better and more efficiently. He's taking time to talk personally to his team when possible, rather than communicating by email. If or when he takes work home it's because he considers it necessary, and not because of wanting to prove his value.

KNOWING YOUR BOUNDARIES

When I refer to addressing our *needs*, I'm talking about recognizing and attending to them; I am *not* talking about feeling sorry for ourselves. There's a strong tendency to be judgmental about ourselves, and to regard having needs as a weakness, when, actually, acknowledging them is a vital part of leadership. As we saw in Chapter 2, this is an obstacle to Business Alchemy. How can we attend to anyone else's needs if we disregard or ignore our own?

Donald Keough, former CEO of the Coca-Cola Company, once said: 'What separates those who achieve from those who do not is in direct proportion to their ability to ask for help.' Throughout every organization there are willing workers with a strong sense of responsibility and the eagerness to get things done. They work hard, for long hours, in response to their workload, wanting to deliver the desired results. But this intensity is simply unsustainable over a long period, and unless it's addressed, it will take its toll.

Taking all the above into consideration, are you overdoing it? Let me ask you:

- 'Do you find yourself resenting some things that go beyond the development of your role?'
- 'Are you acting against your inner voice?'
- 'Do you do what you do because of what you think is expected of you? Or because of what you expect of yourself?'
- 'Is this self-expectation based on what you think others expect of you?'
- 'When you signed up for the job you are in, did you expect to end up doing what you do today?'

- ⚑ 'Did you commit to it then, or has it increased since, disproportionately?'

A little extra time to think: it's self-reflection time! Give yourself the chance to consider the following questions:

- ⚑ 'Am I still enthusiastic about the job I'm doing?'
- ⚑ 'Am I enjoying myself?'
- ⚑ 'Do I have the drive to have fun in my job?'
- ⚑ 'Is there anything missing?'
- ⚑ 'Is there too much of anything?'

A lack of awareness of riding the high-speed train of working long hours – where we give, give and give some more – results from losing sight of what we're supposed to be and do. Daily habits developed unconsciously over years and months will slowly and surely take us away from the track we're supposed to be on. However hard the times we live in, ask yourself this:

> How much value can you add when you are close to collapse? How much support can you give to your team or organization when your brain functions at a fraction of your potential? How long can you keep this up for?

THE ART OF DELEGATION

Micro-management, together with a lack of trust, are the biggest enemies of delegation. I have met great senior leaders who diminish their leadership role by getting their teeth stuck into tasks or detail that someone else could or should be delivering.

A senior executive once told me how sometimes she had to go into a deep level of detail. She was expending more time and energy in doing this than she would have liked, thereby compromising time and energy spent in her key relationships. Through coaching she remembered that diving into things was not part of her job any more; instead, she needed to make sure that the person in charge of that particular detail brought it to her when she needed it.

This is a very basic need, and one that most leaders tend to forget. Although it's sometimes easier to do a task yourself, rather than get it done 'properly or efficiently' by someone else, the habit of diving into things instead of trusting someone else to bring the results to you is costly, in both energy and time. It's often true that to get the right people to deliver what you need requires some investment in time and clear communication, but once a different type of behaviour is established, it will pay off.

Leadership needs vary. Perhaps your need is for straight and clear communication from your boss; for his/her support; to be listened to; for stronger direction; or, for your peers or reports to say 'yes' when they mean 'yes', and 'no' when they mean 'no'. Your need might be the commitment of someone who doesn't report to you, but whose participation is of basic importance to your productivity.

COMMUNICATING REQUESTS EFFECTIVELY

A great teacher once said, 'When I ass-u-me, I make an ass of you and me.' I continually find that most people have a tendency to make assumptions, rather than ask questions in order to gain clarity.

We assume in two ways: when we 'think we know' what *others* want from us, and when we 'take it for granted' that others know what *we* mean and/or what *we* want. We may get it right some of the time, with some of the people around us, but most of the time we're mistaken.

Although there are work descriptions and task distribution methods in most businesses, the lack of clarity surrounding many people's day-to-day work, and the disruption this causes to everybody involved, never ceases to amaze me. Very rarely do expectations match work descriptions, as jobs evolve and tasks are accumulated. Teams, sub-teams or divisions will often hold on to information instead of exchanging it in ways that colleagues would find most helpful for efficiency. This is rarely intentional, but due mostly to doing things automatically, oblivious to whether they work or not.

When we make our own expectations clear, and explain the role or the part that another person plays in our life or work, we establish the basis for discussion and agreement. We can then discuss and negotiate based on what's requested and what's on offer. Reaching agreement implies commitment from both parties to take the consequent responsibility and accountability.

In my experience, too much time and energy in the workplace is wasted due to a lack of clarity concerning what's expected – from us and from others.

The solution is simple: a periodic conversation about expectations is the best way to be sure that you know what your bosses, peers, team members and other work colleagues expect of you. In this way you can agree to deliver, or decline when appropriate.

As a leader of people, it's a useful exercise for you to get your team together and clarify the expectations between the different divisions. It's helpful to do this during a calmer period, and before necessity demands it, whether on your own or with the aid of a coach.

Whether you direct several departments, each with its own leader, or whether you lead a small team, every person in every division will benefit from greater clarity concerning others' needs and expectations. It will prove valuable not only for efficiency and prevention of mistakes, but also for setting boundaries of collaboration between departments, and establishing what can and cannot be delivered.

This will result in a more efficient use of time and resources, as well as a deeper understanding and appreciation of essential needs and priorities, thereby increasing cooperation and commitment across all departments.

Similarly, if you find that members of your direct team are not delivering in the way you want them to, it's important to first clarify your expectations, and second, to ensure that you are giving clear directions with every request.

Requests are effective if they are expressed clearly and include all specific conditions for satisfaction. The expression of agreement and full commitment from the other party is necessary for a successful outcome.

We generally assume when we make a request that the other person will know exactly what we mean. We forget that saying something is often not enough: we also need to 'say it right', by voicing the request in a way and with instructions that the listener will understand, accept and commit to. As George Bernard Shaw put it: 'The problem with communication… is the illusion that it has been accomplished.'

REACHING AGREEMENT

For a request to be effective and be acted on, there needs to be an agreement, or 'contract', on both sides, as in the process of managing expectations. Requests will normally include a 'what', a 'how' and a 'when'.

Sometimes, establishing this new approach to making requests requires a little patience. If you're used to rushing from one task to the next, you need to take time to be in the state of mind necessary to create the new behaviour – or to allow time for your team members to become proficient in this process. It's important for your team members to understand that, should you omit any of the specific conditions necessary for them to satisfy your request (such as 'what', 'how', 'where' or 'when'), you expect *them* to ask for the information before committing to delivering the result.

It sounds basic, but this is largely overlooked in business. Once we know people's expectations, and they know ours, this process can become shorter and faster. Any time you want to know where you stand in a situation, it's a good moment to revisit the process of reaching agreement.

THE WEAK, HOT-TEMPERED LEADER

There is, of course, a type of leader who is so focused on his or her role, objectives and own speed, that he or she ends up frustrated. This type of leader expects everyone on the team to work to his or her high speed and standards, forgetting to check others' qualities and skills. A culture of tension or hot-temperedness is often the result, as this story demonstrates:

⟿ BUSINESS ALCHEMY IN ACTION ⟻

The managing director of an organization had been in his position for one year. For the first few months he pushed the whole management team very enthusiastically, to bring on changes that he considered vital for the growth and achievement of the company. A man with a history of significant results, he had a clear vision of what he wanted to achieve.

He worked around the clock, did not sleep much, and had little time for family and friends. He started sending emails at 6 a.m. and was still sending emails at 11 p.m. every weekday; not to mention the emails he sent at weekends now and again. In his sheer determination to achieve what he set out to achieve, he was not *managing* his people but *bullying* them into action. However charming and at ease he could be when things went his way, he ruled by fear and was oblivious to the corroding self-confidence in his team.

This leader did not accept any feedback concerning things that might not work; he shouted at people and called them stupid when they didn't act or function at his speed or to his standards. He completely lost sight of the bare necessities of both himself and his people. It might seem that he was attending to his own needs, since he was attending only to his own priorities, but, whether he wanted to prove that he was the right man for the job, or whether he simply wanted to achieve what he'd committed to for the stakeholders, he overlooked his strong need for a motivated and effective team, as well as his basic needs for sleep and rest.

In the meantime, while he was paying attention only to the lower needs of his ego – misusing power to get his team to work his way and at his pace – 50 per cent of the senior executives in his team left the company. Other board members were on the verge of leaving, too, and others feared their own response if this man's aggression came their way.

How long could he go on like this? His aim was to make a difference and he was making a difference for sure, but was this the difference he *wanted* to make? Could he pay such a price?

When we look at the lenses, we see that this leader was clearly so driven by task and results that he was blind to anything and anyone else. Emotional discontent is the biggest waste of time and effort I have encountered in the 24 years of my career.

Although this style of leadership is still very much present in certain industries, it's generally on its way out, due to the difficulty of maintaining its efficiency. In today's organizations, people are no longer willing to put up with it. When targets are long term and the work atmosphere is tense, the cost of staff turnover, especially at leadership level, proves too expensive.

It's a characteristic of weak leadership to attend solely to short-term needs and live unremittingly in emergency mode (firefighting). It's the equivalent of driving with the positional lights on all the way. Eventually we need to switch to long-distance lights to see the road. In a similar manner, it's important to look further ahead on the road of leadership – not only to prevent accidents, but also to allow room for flexibility in case of hold-ups. It's vital to look long term to prioritize accordingly and prevent future fires.

Leaders are becoming more open and balanced. They keep an eye on targets while also looking after their staff. They attend to the needs of the organization. Their priority – and their need – is retaining talent. New-generation leaders create Business Alchemy.

~ 12 ~

THE ART OF EFFECTIVE FEEDBACK

There is no failure, only feedback.

NLP presupposition

The direct relationship between feedback and performance is now well established. However, for it to be truly effective, the feedback has to be given in the most clear and impactful manner.

In this chapter we look at the power of feedback and its effect on performance; we look at the essential elements of feedback necessary for it to be effective, and we see how to give unpleasant feedback as well as pleasant facts.

Since feedback is the key to making a constructive impact and helping to develop your team, this chapter starts by diving in to an explanation of all the aspects involved, so ensuring that they become second nature. It's only when we embrace these elements as natural and ever present that we master the art of feedback.

The most important thing to remember during Alchemic conversations, as in any other enterprise, is your *intention*: your goal or desired outcome. Contrary to what some people suppose, the intention of feedback is not just saying what we think but:

- Encouraging authenticity and self-confidence.
- Developing awareness, responsibility and commitment.
- Sponsoring your team by providing recognition.

The ability to address your team while incorporating the three points above will ensure improved quality of communication, and a pleasing flow to your conversations, whether managing progress or during feedback on the spot.

ENCOURAGING AUTHENTICITY AND SELF-CONFIDENCE

Self-esteem has a strong impact on an individual's performance and achievement of goals; it also has an important effect on their attitude towards hierarchy and the ability to 'manage upwards'. When you enable your team members to strengthen their belief in their own competence, they associate their newfound state with you.

It's the most effective way for you to enhance their self-confidence because it encourages them to trust themselves to follow their own initiative more often. The 'feelgood factor' of being confident and delivering good results will increase their personal appreciation, and the likelihood of them wanting to follow you and engage in your endeavours.

Eleanor Roosevelt once said, 'No one can make you feel inferior without your consent.' However, as we saw in Chapter 3, it's also true to say that certain ways of talking to people are more likely to trigger deep emotional reactions that result in negative choices.

As a leader, you have a significant impact on your team's perception of their competence. If a leader has the effect of *shredding* an individual's self-esteem, that person's productivity and performance level are negatively impacted.

In contrast, if the leader's contributions *boost* the individual's self-esteem, that person's motivation to perform well increases, as does their self-confidence, therefore creating an engaging circle of competence.

Most of us are motivated to work at the level we perceive we are competent. A team member who feels capable is much more likely to perform more competently than one who feels incompetent (and is likely to act with caution and underperform).

Following are examples of statements that could trigger a drop in confidence levels and self-esteem, since they could be considered patronizing and confronting to the ego and result in a defensive response that's counterproductive.

- ▱ 'This project may be too complex for you.'

- ▱ 'Let's see if you are capable of doing it right
  this time.'

- ▱ 'This is the second time we've discussed your
  relationship with your team. I don't intend to discuss
  it again.'

And here are some examples of statements that help to *build* confidence and self-esteem, since they appeal to the individual's creativity and recognition:

- ▱ 'What are your ideas for improving your level of
  influence over your stakeholders?'

- ▱ 'You're 15 per cent over budget for this project. How
  can we bring the costs under control?'

- ▱ 'Last time we spoke, you said you felt that an 8
  per cent increase in productivity was reasonable.
  However, so far this department is at 2 per cent.
  What's happened since we last reviewed this issue?'

EXERCISE: BOOSTING PEOPLE'S CONFIDENCE

~~~

You may be naturally adept at boosting people's confidence, or you may need a little practice at it. Remember, if you believe in your people, you'll say the right things to them. Think about the questions below and note your response.

- ⌁ What have you heard or seen other leaders say or do – or what have you said or done – to enhance others' self-esteem? *Be specific.*

- ⌁ What have you heard or seen other leaders say or do that has intentionally or unintentionally lowered others' self-esteem? *Be specific.*

- ⌁ How could these be changed to boost self-esteem?

Now think about someone in your team who might benefit from your 'boosting' comments. What could you say, however briefly, that would make a difference to their perception of themselves?

＞＞＞

When we believe that the person in front of us has all the resources they need, we automatically ask the right questions to extract what's inside them. When we believe in people, it's evident, and it becomes infectious. It acts as a trigger so they start to believe it themselves.

If for any reason you *don't* believe that the person in front of you has the necessary internal resources to do what you expect them to do (or you don't believe they can access them), I invite you to check whether this is *truly* because of their level of competence and ability, or whether it has more to do with your own preconceptions. This perception could even be due to the different choice of lenses between you, and therefore your different perspectives (see Chapter 6).

I encourage you now to experiment and tell yourself you are going to believe in them *just this once*. Follow the process *as if* you believe. Then watch the consequences.

DEVELOPING AWARENESS, RESPONSIBILITY AND COMMITMENT

Feedback is used to help develop awareness of habits, attitudes or behaviour that the person in question may or may not be aware of; it enables him or her to take responsibility for doing what would be pertinent to change that behaviour.

There are several factors to take into consideration when giving feedback.

Check Your Own Emotional State

Before any feedback is given, it's of paramount importance that you are in a stable emotional state and keep in mind the intention or desired outcome of the feedback. Remember, feedback is not a tool for you to let out any kind of frustration on the individual, or to show your disappointment, but an instrument for improving future performance. Therefore, it's imperative that you put your emotions aside and be as objective as possible.

Providing feedback when deeply irritated, angry or upset about something will be counterproductive. If necessary, remove yourself physically from the situation until you have composed yourself. This could be a good time to consider the lenses that you are both using. It will help when evaluating the person's skills and behaviour.

Focus on Specific Behaviour

For feedback to be effective, you need to talk about *behaviour* – avoid making a vague statement about the person. Be clear and specific about what someone is *doing or saying*. Speaking in a matter-of-fact fashion puts the focus directly onto the person's behaviour or actions, and their immediate consequence.

If, instead, you focus on attitude or personality, the statement will either be too vague and ambiguous to increase awareness, or likely to provoke defensiveness and rejection, in some cases triggering deep resentment that will have a negative impact on overall performance. Therefore, communicate clearly and effectively, and focus on the specifics of what the team member is, or is not, doing or saying.

For example, rather than saying: 'Your lack of commitment caused the whole project to fail', it's more effective to say: 'Luke, you agreed to complete the task by Thursday. The deadline was missed by two days.'

Focusing on *impact* means recognizing how the specific behaviour affects others or the environment: the domino effect. For example, poor documentation can affect others who rely on that documentation for accuracy in the future. Focusing on the impact of specific behaviour helps the direct report see the importance of taking responsibility for addressing that behaviour.

For example: 'Luke, you agreed to complete the task by Thursday. The deadline was missed by two days and therefore the team was unable to complete the project on time. Our client is clearly unsatisfied and the department's reputation is in jeopardy.'

Using feedback that focuses on specific behaviour and its impact, rather than on personality or attitude, will maintain the report's self-esteem. This position combines correction of behaviour with constructive criticism.

EXERCISE: DESCRIBING SPECIFIC
BEHAVIOUR AND IMPACT
~~~

In the statements below, the boss has given vague remarks that the employee cannot or will not make sense of. *This occurrence is more common than we dare to think.*

Take a little time to rethink each of the statements and *rewrite them*, describing any specific behaviour and impact that would fit the vague description given.

 ⇉ 'Heather, I don't know what has happened to your attitude. You used to be great when it came to dealing with new customers, but now your attitude towards them has gone downhill. That has to change.'

(This is a vague description that means nothing to Heather. Beginning by asking a question about how Heather thinks her attitude impacted on the new customer would encourage her to take responsibility for her choice of behaviour.)

 ⇉ 'Terry, you just don't show enough initiative. Increasing your initiative has to become a high priority for you now.'

(Again, in this example the feedback says nothing of what happened and makes it difficult for Terry to know what's meant by the remark. How is 'initiative' to be assessed or measured?)

    ⌐ 'Teamwork is critical to success here, Gary, and I suggest
    you work on becoming more of a team player.'

(This style of comment is used far too often. It means nothing.
It doesn't help Gary to understand that he has been working in
isolation, or what he needs to do to become more of a team player.
In the worst-case scenario, it could even have the contrary effect
of reinforcing his sense that he is 'outside' the team.)

~~~

GIVING EFFECTIVE FEEDBACK

There are three key steps in this process:

1. Describe the Situation (What and When)

What were the circumstances at the time? What was going
on? When?

2. Describe the Specific Behaviour

What, specifically, was he/she doing? What are the verbal and
non-verbal actions that you wish to reinforce, or need to be
changed/improved?

3. Describe the Impact

What was the impact or consequence (the domino effect) of
this behaviour on you, on others, on the person's results, the
team goals, the department, the sales, etc?

SPONSORING YOUR TEAM BY PROVIDING RECOGNITION

Providing recognition is a confidence-builder that helps the
receiver to gain awareness of what does and doesn't work. It

also enhances their future ability to take responsibility for their choice of behaviour.

The Benefits of Providing Recognition:

- It provides positive feedback to acknowledge and reward good performance.

- It reinforces good work and shapes future behaviour.

- It's a powerful motivator

- It builds trust.

- It builds self-esteem and confidence.

- It makes people more receptive to feedback, thus improving performance.

It's Important to Provide Recognition When a Report:

- Does something that you would like him/her to repeat.

- Accomplishes something that was difficult for him/her.

- Meets or exceeds his/her goals; completes a development goal.

- Demonstrates a competency effectively.

- Shows initiative in coming up with innovative ideas or in solving problems.

- Goes the extra mile.

- Takes appropriate action to support organizational/ work unit/team plans and goals.

⊯ Takes a prudent risk.

⊯ Makes progress in learning and demonstrating new skills or knowledge.

⊯ Achieves a milestone in pursuing a long-term or complex plan or goal.

⊯ Improves his/her performance.

HOW TO PROVIDE RECOGNITION

Consider the recognition/feedback given below. What do you think of it?

'Hey, Jim, I noticed your productivity is way up. Keep up the good work.'

Recognition is feedback, and although Jim will have a temporary boost from what could be a positive comment, the truth is that the statement is not meaningful. It needs further explanation. Providing recognition is a way of providing feedback; therefore it's important to follow the three steps we followed for feedback (above). Getting into the habit of using the three steps makes the process of coaching-style conversations simple and impactful.

1. Describe the Situation (What and When)

First, make a general statement about the performance being recognized. For example: 'You've made a very effective presentation to the customer...'

2. Describe the Specific Behaviour

Then describe specifically what he/she said or did (specific behaviour) that contributed to the positive results. For example: 'You spoke slowly and clearly and stated all the benefits for both sides very eloquently. You also had all the answers they wanted...'.

3. Describe the Impact

Finally, describe how the person's performance positively impacted his, her, or the team's performance. For example: 'The customer has decided to work with us and has placed an order.'

Be specific about what the person did effectively, and *when* and *why* it was effective (the positive impact – on their results, on others' results, on customers/stockholders, on other people, on the department/organization). Remember the following:

- Recognition must be sincere, succinct and specific.
- You need to 'catch people doing something right'.
- Consider using diverse forms of recognition that suit your personality: it's essential to be genuine.

EXERCISE: PRACTISING RECOGNITION

In your own time, think about and identify a report who did something recently that deserves recognition.

Using the three-step format, determine what you would say to him/her to provide recognition, and describe the impact of his/her effective performance:

⌐ Describe the *situation* (what and when).

⌐ Describe the specific *behaviour.*

⌐ Describe the positive *impact,* however small.

~~~

It's not necessary for the impact to be talked about every time, since some of your reports will be more acquainted with the effect of their actions than others. Bear in mind too, that the level of specific detail you need to give will depend on whether your report has a preference for the Picture or the Detail lens.

Let's now revisit the recognition given to Jim earlier: 'Hey, Jim, I noticed your productivity is way up. Keep up the good work.'

There are several situations in which a passing comment like this can be made. It could either imply a history of 'knowing' between Jim and his boss, or it could indicate a very hands-off leadership style. This particular remark could be constructive if made in the context of a follow-up about a subject that Jim and his boss have spoken of as one of Jim's goals: providing they also find five minutes another time to go over the specifics.

However, in other circumstances the remark could be unhelpful, and could be received as patronizing: it doesn't invite an exchange of knowledge, or a deeper understanding of what behaviour has improved Jim's productivity.

⌐ What could you say that would make the comment more authentic?

◿ What specific behaviours could make this statement more credible?

FEEDBACK IN A NUTSHELL

Feedback is the process of giving others information about what they're doing effectively (performance and behaviour), and what they could do differently – to better meet expectations, to be more effective, or to improve future performance results.

The Benefits of Feedback:

◿ It ensures continuous improvement.

◿ It clarifies performance expectations.

◿ It develops reports' knowledge, skills, and performance.

◿ It builds productive working relationships.

◿ It encourages reports to take responsibility.

◿ It promotes awareness.

It's important that feedback is objective and delivered in the right frame of mind.

Feedback is Most Effective When it's:

◿ Given in the right emotional and mental state

◿ Focused on behaviour within the report's control

◿ Selective, i.e. focused on one or two important issues rather than on several issues

- Describing *behaviour* rather than evaluating or judging the person

- Specific

- Prompt rather than delayed

- Done in a way that encourages two-way communication

- Collaborative with regard to a solution

- Focused towards the future, not the past

CONCLUSION: THE IMPACT OF BUSINESS ALCHEMY

'The ultimate step in leadership is growing from being convincing to being enamouring.'

Erik Larsson

Recently I was sitting with a former leader-client, Erik Larsson, during a triangular coaching session, discussing the growth road for one of his direct reports. Erik explained how, four years earlier, he'd been the one in the hot seat, working with me on his leadership development. As he spoke about all the things we'd worked on, and explained his leadership journey, Erik was being open and sincere, accepting his vulnerability with great humour. I found him mesmerizing.

I feel privileged to have witnessed his transition from a very talented professional – rational, logical, serious, and an unexciting communicator, like many others – into a genuinely charismatic and engaging leader. I saw how he'd achieved the stage of personal authenticity, and how he'd moved from *thinking* he had to be convincing to *actually being* a warm, wholehearted and clear communicator.

He enthused others not only to fall in love with his vision, but to follow him and want to participate in it. Today, more than ever, Erik is influencing his people and his business, and consequently his industry.

Throughout *The Business Alchemist* we have seen genuine stories from leaders who, like Erik, have experienced this transformation in their own skin. Senior executives have kindly shared with us how embracing the leadership journey to the full has played a role in their personal growth – raising their leadership bar to the next level.

Their first-hand experiences explain how they altered their view of themselves and the world, thus expanding their understanding of relationships, their boundaries, and their effectiveness in engaging with their team, their peers and their bosses. Their journeys to the soul of leadership have had a direct impact on their private as well as their professional lives. Here, senior healthcare professional Tracey McNeill shares her leadership journey.

~ BUSINESS ALCHEMY IN ACTION ~

As I begin to write this, it's hard to believe that, despite a lifetime in healthcare management – often at a senior level – how my approach and therefore execution of leadership has changed. This was in part due to my moving to a global social business/charity as a vice president, effectively a CEO role for the first time, but in the main down to being provided with an executive coach (the first time that this has been offered to me in over 30 years of management).

So, less than two years ago, I met Pilar. Little did I know at that point the profound effect she would have, not just on me but those around me. Quite amazingly Pilar was able to understand how I worked, what made me tick, and that I worked through people and strove to be authentic. She would ask me 'What do you want to talk about today?' and I would explain some particularly difficult situation – it might be working with my peers, the global CEO or even the Board.

Pilar helped take me to places I'd never been brave enough to go. She helped me become focused on an issue and find a solution that was right for me and right for the organization. She has an incredible insight into people and situations; she helped me see a problem through the eyes of others, and how they worked, and therefore which buttons to push and push them harder than I would have done before.

Now, two years later, I am a better, more authentic leader. I used to wallow in getting to where I needed to; now I can get there faster and smarter. I don't waste time on non-issues – I know what I want and I get there. Most importantly, the organization is in a better place. But it has helped in every aspect of my life, guiding our teenage children, helping friends who are making difficult decisions, negotiating with my husband! I see life differently now.

These stories summarize the message in this book; namely:

- A Business Alchemist is an inspiring, excellent and outstanding leader.

- A Business Alchemist makes time to think about long-term strategy, and dares to plan for the effort of implementing it.

- Excellent leaders have a good relationship with risk; this is due to their confidence in Self and trusting not only their knowledge but also their Wisdom.

- If you are prepared to put in the effort it entails, you can also become an excellent, authentic leader and a Business Alchemist.

- By daring to be authentic, you will improve your life, your business and your contribution to the world.

TAKING RISKS: MOVING BUSINESS FURTHER

It's a quality of leadership to create chaos so as to find a new level of stability, but most leaders resist change. They fail to take enough perspective to see beyond the short- and middle-term company objectives: as I explained in the introduction, they look at half a rainbow, conform to half a beauty.

It's easy for leaders to get lost in the busy day-to-day, and continue to do things the way they've always done them because it works. Sometimes they don't find the right time for putting in the effort and enduring the upheaval that the required change might entail. While this might have helped them survive so far, it's not what's called for in times of crisis. Now, more than ever, we need excellent and courageous leaders who dare to take the business further.

Cynthia Montgomery, immediate former head of the Strategy Unit at Harvard Business School in the USA, writes the following in the conclusion to her book *The Strategist*:

> *'Behind every pulsating, vibrant, successful strategy is a leader who seized the initiative and made it happen. Developing and executing strategy with all the necessary dimensions, including the accountability that attends to making decisions with great consequence, is not a function, it is a leadership job, and a big one.'*

Cynthia's words highlight the essence of this book: we both see the need to add the leadership dimension to the strategist and executive roles. For this to happen, we need to look at the leadership excellence of the Business Alchemist.

Today's businesses need leaders who have developed to the leadership platform where the ego works harmoniously with the soul. Leaders who understand not only business and strategy, but also people – their needs, preferences, motivations and fears – and who dare to take the risk of creating chaos when it's necessary. Leaders who look beyond the middle or even long-term strategy and contribute to the development not only of their business, but of their industry.

As Business Alchemists we know we can serve our team in supporting them with what they need to deliver and contribute to the full. By opening our minds to possibilities, thoughts and beliefs that empower us and support our chosen direction, *we* shape the quality of our experiences or our reality.

This theory is supported by the findings of the biologist and research scientist Dr Bruce Lipton, who carried out an experiment in which he put identical sets of cells on different plates and observed their growth in different environments. He found that the cells, although comprised of the same DNA, evolved differently depending on the beneficial or destructive energy of the environments they were exposed to, including the impulses radiating from our thoughts.

When we modify our thoughts and/or our perception of the world, we change our experience of life. By experiencing life differently we make different choices and live in a more empowering way, thus achieving greater fulfilment.

We can apply our thoughts by allowing ourselves to be who we truly are; accepting that the more authentic we are, the more value we add to ourselves and others. We don't need to change ourselves, but to change the *perception* we hold of ourselves, therefore accepting and growing out of our shortcomings and embracing and celebrating our uniqueness and our gifts.

The Business Alchemist is a wonderful invitation to be our own true Self, leaving aside the fear of not complying with the world around us. If we ignore our true value, talents, skills and feelings, we will jeopardize our impact, and risk depriving the world around us of the benefit of our uniqueness. By modifying our view of ourselves and our surroundings, we transform our world and our lives.

Throughout this book we've looked at how our past thoughts and beliefs have brought us to where we are today. We are in charge of choosing empowering thoughts and beliefs, so that we can use the present to steer towards our desired future. In the end, it's the journey towards excellence that nourishes who we are, and our experience of it that puts us in touch with our inner voice and Wisdom.

YOUR LEGACY AS A LEADER AND A PERSON

It's during this journey that we are most likely to get in touch with our mission and meaning in life. As I mentioned earlier, I've found life's purpose to be altruistic. Of the hundreds of people I've worked with over the years, every one of them has revealed their life's purpose to be about service to others.

Have you, at some moment during your life – whether some time ago or recently – wondered what life is all about? What are you doing here? What is the reason or the purpose of your passage here on Earth?

I think most of us have thought about this, but we might choose to get on with life and forget about such enquiry, or leave the question open in the hope of finding the answer some day. Some of us, however, have found the answer.

I've always worked to help clients connect with their purpose as far as they are ready to do so. Some years ago I had confirmation of the successful business impact of this connection, when, within the coaching commission of one of the global companies I was working with, the first target was to help the leader to find *his or her life purpose* – or at least set them on the right path to finding it.

Finding this connection helps to shape the platform of leadership we're aiming at, and sets a new intensity of force and drive towards searching and delivering organizational targets, while serving the individual's personal targets and their soul.

On this subject, during the course of coaching, I bring to my clients the following scenario, which I now also share with you.

When I am 94 I shall host a birthday party, to which you are invited. I would like you to bring me a gift, and that gift will be your answer to these questions.

- 'What have you done with your life that you are most proud of?'
- 'What will be your legacy?'

(These answers are not to include your children – who one day will want to do something to be proud of – but your contribution to the world.)

I help my clients to get to the answers to these questions by talking first about themselves, and then about their business. I ask them the following:

First of all, concentrate on you as a person.

- What do I bring or want to bring more into the world?

- What difference do I make?

- What is my *unique* contribution to my business, my people and my life?

- Am I doing today what I need to do in life? If not, what do I intend to do about it? What is my plan?

- How committed am I to making a difference with my contribution to the world?

When I spoke earlier about short- or middle-term strategy, I was referring to the fact that, as a leader in an organization, it's easy to concentrate mainly on what the market is doing, or on planning and implementing a new strategy to grow the business. This can distract us from looking beyond the business targets into a broader view so that we can see it as part of a greater vision. Since you might be interested in looking beyond and into the greater vision, let's ask similar questions to those about *your business.*

- What does my business bring or want to bring more into the world?

- What difference does it make?

- What is its unique contribution to the industry, to people and to the world?

- Are we as an organization doing today what we need to do so that we'll still be significant tomorrow? If not, what do we intend to do about it?

- How committed are we to making a difference with our contribution to the world?

After finding the general idea of the subject above, you'll be closer to finding the answers to the earlier questions.

- When you come to my 94th birthday party, what will you tell me you've done in your life that you're most proud of?
- What legacy will you want to leave behind?

Earlier in the book I talked about the universal motivators of Recognition and Belonging. Of course, most leaders are motivated by ambition, but what's to be gained ultimately by such ambition? Not money, not power or status – but meaning.

To know the purpose of our existence is the ultimate motivator. Once we find our life's purpose we don't need any other incentive. We automatically alter our needs and priorities and raise our energy to serve our purpose by whatever means possible. This makes our leadership, our work, our relationships and our lives the vehicle for something far greater.

Finally, one of my clients who *has* found the answer to the questions above writes:

~ BUSINESS ALCHEMY IN ACTION ~

In becoming a Business Alchemist I've taken a journey that has put me in touch with my deepest motivation and life's purpose. It has also led me to connect my personal with my professional purpose in a surprising and deep way.

This has opened up my vision of my role as a leader, and built strong long-term commitment to serving my purpose through leadership. The whole experience has been about reaching congruence and alignment, about personal growth, about finding myself and my unique contribution to the world.

⇜ ACKNOWLEDGEMENTS ⇝

With gratitude.

When I first set out to write *The Business Alchemist* I had a different book in mind to the one that you have in your hands. Needless to say, the final product is a much more proficient and beautiful book than I imagined, and it wouldn't have been like this had it not been for the essential participation of Sarah Sutton, Sue Blake, Piet Gruwez and my beautiful clients who have generously shared their stories with you.

Special thanks to Sarah Sutton, who patiently helped me with writing in 'proper' English all the way through, and stuck with me through the painful periods.

To Piet Gruwez, who took time out of his crazy schedule as a VP for Marketing and Sales of a global organization to read each chapter and give me feedback from the point of view of both the executive leader and the general reader, adding relevance to the text.

To Sue Blake, for putting me in touch with the right people in the book industry, and for the inspiring brainstorming sessions and constant support.

I also want to thank each and every leader I have coached for helping me learn about leadership from the witness's chair, and for inspiring me with their progress. To all the Business Alchemists I have come in contact with.

I'm grateful to Sheila Crowley at Curtis Brown for taking me on board and finding Hay House; and to Carolyn Thorne and the team at Hay House for their trust and support.

To Daryl Jelinek for taking the time to read the book in the thick of organizing the Olympics, and for providing a quote for the cover.

Special thanks to Robert Dilts, not only for the foreword, but also for his continuous support throughout the years; and to creators and developers of NLP, on which some of the models in this book are based.

Very personal thanks to my children, Gavin and Vivien, for celebrating each milestone with me, and for sometimes sorting out dinner so I could carry on writing.

Lastly, to all of you who embark on the journey to becoming a Business Alchemist, for your courage in wanting to grow. Without you this book would have no purpose.

JOIN THE HAY HOUSE FAMILY

As the leading self-help, mind, body and spirit publisher in the UK, we'd like to welcome you to our family so that you can enjoy all the benefits our website has to offer.

 EXTRACTS from a selection of your favourite author titles

 COMPETITIONS, PRIZES & SPECIAL OFFERS Win extracts, money off, downloads and so much more

 LISTEN to a range of radio interviews and our latest audio publications

 CELEBRATE YOUR BIRTHDAY An inspiring gift will be sent your way

 LATEST NEWS Keep up with the latest news from and about our authors

 **ATTEND OUR AUTHOR EVENTS** Be the first to hear about our author events

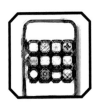 **iPHONE APPS** Download your favourite app for your iPhone

 HAY HOUSE INFORMATION Ask us anything, all enquiries answered

join us online at **www.hayhouse.co.uk**

 Astley House, 33 Notting Hill Gate, London W11 3JQ
T: 020 3675 2450 E: info@hayhouse.co.uk

ABOUT THE AUTHOR

Pilar Godino is an internationally acclaimed leadership coach whose extensive experience and consistently successful results have established her as one of the pre-eminent individuals in her profession, in a career spanning over 20 years.

Her clients include major corporations such as Diageo, Accenture, Danone, PepsiCo, Heineken, Vesuvius and ING, as well as the European Union and various non-governmental organizations. Pilar works at senior executive level and specializes in transformational leadership and Executive Team Performance within multicultural environments. *Personal Impact*™ *Coaching*, Pilar's unique methodology, combines leadership coaching with elements of Neuro-Linguistic Programming (NLP) in a dynamic blend that brings about fast and profound change. Her methods have been described by many clients as 'Alchemy in action'.

Pilar was one of the first coaches in Europe to be awarded the position of Master Certified Coach by the International Coaching Federation (ICF). Most recently she was advisor at the Centre of Expertise on Coaching (CEC) at the international Vlerick Leuven Gent Management School in Belgium, and was invited to collaborate with the programme's creative team.

Pilar also runs NLP-related leadership seminars internationally, sometimes partnering with other leading professionals such as Robert Dilts. Qualified as a Success Factor Coach by the NLP University in California and a Neuro Semantics Practitioner, Pilar has developed new models and methodology in the fields of NLP and coaching.

She has more than 7,000 hours of coaching practice, and over 12,000 hours of experience in the field of Personal Development, and clients find her dynamic, supportive, inspiring, challenging, transparent, insightful, and with great humour.

www.pilargodino.com

CPSIA information can be obtained at www.ICGtesting.com
Printed in the USA
BVOW070113080313

315011BV00001B/2/P